NON-FUNGIBLE TOKEN (NFT) INVESTING MASTERY - CRYPTOCURRENCY HISTORY, MARKET ANALYSIS, CREATE, MARKET, BUY, SELL AND TRADE

NFT Crypto Investing Guide for Beginners to Expert: Art, Tokens, Music, Film

CAMERON BELFORD

Silk Publishing

INTRODUCTION

I am very excited about the prospect of using cryptocurrency, not just as a money equivalent, but using it as a way to earn something as a result of doing some type of work.

— WILLIAM MOUGAYAR

NFTs (non-fungible tokens) is a kind of cryptocurrency asset where each item, or token, is unique. As a result, they are useless as a currency but extremely useful for other purposes, such as crypto art. Crypto art is digital work of art associated with unique tokens (or NFTs). NFTs work in the same way as cryptographic tokens, but unlike cryptos like Bitcoin, they are neither interchangeable nor fungible. Instead, a chain of identifiable data blocks is created when blockchains string records of cryptographic hash, a collection of characters that verifies a piece of data to be genuine, onto previous records.

This book will teach you everything you need to know

about non-fungible tokens, including using cryptocurrency in blockchain to buy, sell, and invest in NFT crypto.

A BRIEF ABOUT THE
BLOCKCHAIN

Blockchain may appear complicated, and it can be, but its underlying notion is extremely simple. A blockchain is essentially a form of database. Therefore, to comprehend blockchain, it is necessary to first grasp what a database is.

A database is a collection of data that is electronically stored on a computer system. Database information, or data, is often organized in table style to facilitate searching and filtering for specific information. What is the difference between storing information in a spreadsheet versus a database?

Spreadsheets are intended for storing and accessing limited amounts of information by a single person or a small group of individuals. On the other hand, a database is intended to contain substantially larger volumes of information that can be accessed, filtered, and changed rapidly and simply by any number of users at the same time.

Large databases do this by storing data on servers comprised of powerful computers. These servers can occasionally be built with hundreds or thousands of processors to provide the computing power and storage capacity required for several users to access the database simultaneously. While anybody can access a spreadsheet or database, it is usually owned by a business and maintained by an assigned individual who has complete control over how it functions and the data contained inside it.

MAJOR DIFFERENCE BETWEEN BLOCKCHAIN AND A DATABASE

Structure of data

The primary distinction between blockchain and a database is the storage structure. The way data is structured in a traditional database and a blockchain differs significantly. A blockchain collects information in groups known as blocks, which include sets of data. When a block is filled, it is chained onto the previously filled block, producing a data chain known as the "blockchain." All new information that follows that newly added block is combined into a newly formed block, which is then added to the chain once full.

A database organizes data into tables, whereas a blockchain, as the name suggests, organizes data into chunks (blocks) that are chained together. As a result, while all blockchains are databases, not all databases are blockchains. When implemented in a decentralized manner, this method creates an irreversible data timeline. When a block is completed, it is imprinted in stone and becomes a part of this timeline. When a block is added to the chain, it is assigned a precise timestamp.

Decentralized Nature

To understand it, it is helpful to view blockchain from how Bitcoin has implemented it. Bitcoin, like a database, requires a collection of computers to store its blockchain. This blockchain is simply a form of database that keeps every Bitcoin transaction ever made. In the case of Bitcoin, and unlike most databases, these computers are not all housed under the same roof, and each computer or group of computers is run by a distinct individual or group of individuals.

Assume a corporation owns a server with 10,000 computers and a database containing its clients' account information. In addition, this corporation has a warehouse where all of these computers are housed under one roof. Thus, it has complete authority over all of these systems and the information contained within them. Similarly, Bitcoin is made up of thousands of computers. Still, each computer or group of computers that holds its blockchain is located in a different geographic area and is run by different persons or groups of people. Nodes are the computers that makeup Bitcoin's network.

The blockchain of Bitcoin is used decentralizedly in this paradigm. However, private, centralized blockchains exist, in which the machines that comprise the network are owned and maintained by a single company.

Each node in a blockchain contains a complete record of the data that has been stored on the blockchain from its start. Thus, the data for Bitcoin is the whole history of all Bitcoin transactions. If a node's data has an error, it can use the thousands of other nodes as a reference point to rectify itself. In this manner, no single node in the network may change the information stored within it. As a result, the history of transactions in each block of Bitcoin's blockchain is irreversible.

If a single user tampers with Bitcoin's transaction record, the other nodes will cross-reference each other and readily identify the node with inaccurate information. This system aids in the establishment of an exact and visible sequence of occurrences. This information is a list of transactions for Bitcoin; however, a blockchain can also include various information such as legal contracts, state identifications, or a company's product inventory.

To change how that system functions or the information stored within it, most of the processing power in the decentralized network must agree on the modifications. This ensures that any changes that are implemented are in the best interests of the majority.

HISTORY OF BLOCKCHAIN

The blockchain concept was first described in 1991 by Stuart Haber, and W. Scott Stornetta's full name is Scott Stornetta. They want to provide a computationally feasible approach for timestamping digital documents to prevent them from being backdated or tampered with. They create a method for storing timestamped documents that use the notion of a cryptographically protected chain of blocks.

Merkle Trees were integrated into the architecture in 1992, making blockchain more efficient by enabling several documents to be aggregated into a single block. Merkle Trees are used to establish a "secured chain of blocks." It stores a sequence of data entries, each of which is linked to the one before it. The most recent record in this chain covers the whole chain's history. However, the technique was never implemented, and the patent expired in 2004.

Hal Finney, a computer scientist and cryptography campaigner, presented Reusable Proof Of Work (RPoW) as a prototype for digital cash in 2004. It was a critical early milestone in cryptocurrency history. The RPoW system functioned by obtaining a non-exchangeable or non-fungible Hashcash-based proof of work token in exchange for an RSA-signed token, which could then be passed from person to person.

RPoW fixed the double-spending issue by registering token ownership on a trustworthy server. This server was created to enable people all around the globe to verify its accuracy and integrity in real-time.

Satoshi Nakamoto also theorized the principle of distributed blockchains in 2008. He enhances the concept in a novel manner, allowing blocks to be added to the original chain without being signed by trustworthy parties. The updated trees would keep a secure record of data transfers. It timestamps and verifies each trade via a peer-to-peer network. It may be administered independently, without the need for a centralized authority. Because of these advancements, blockchains have become the backbone of cryptocurrencies. Today, the design acts as the public record for all Bitcoin transactions.

Blockchain progress has been steady and promising. The terms block and chain were used independently in Satoshi Nakamoto's original paper, but they were subsequently popularized as one phrase, blockchain, by 2016. In addition, the file size of the Bitcoin blockchain, which contains records of all transactions that have happened on the network, has just increased from 20 GB to 100 GB.

BLOCKCHAIN-BASED NON-FUNGIBLE TOKENS

Without getting too off course, you can consider blockchain as a monstrous expert duplicate of an accounting page to which anybody can add a line of data, for example, the unique ID of an NFT appended to a piece of crypto craftsmanship.

The blockchain can confirm verification of responsible for advanced resources by checking it against this book-keeping page. This accounting page makes it almost difficult to degrade the data since all PCs check this bookkeeping page against one another to confirm what is unique or phony. Think about this another way: To check Picasso's credibility, you need an artistic workmaster who comprehends the piece's set of experiences from one authority to another. In the crypto world, the blockchain is somewhat similar to the artistic workmaster. Crypto craftsmanship lives on its blockchain called Ethereum blockchain—more on that later.

The advantages to trading advanced craftsmanship on blockchain are very much like those of cryptographic trading money. It is an elective technique—and as indicated exactly, an unrivaled one—to claiming advanced artistry and confirming it. Similarly, as the indistinguishable records ensure Bitcoin exchanges' security, computerized artisans can expect greater security and higher incentive for work that is exchanged on a blockchain. Verisart is a Blockchain check stage for specialists.

BLOCKCHAIN VERSUS CRYPTOCURRENCY

Blockchains are cryptographically secure distributed ledgers. They are essentially public databases that anybody may contribute to or examine at any time. Instead of storing data on a single centralized server, the data is replicated over thousands and thousands of computers worldwide, allowing each machine to access this database. Transactions are aggregated into data-holding units called "blocks." A blockchain is a distributed database of chronologically ordered transactions comprised of the consecutive string of every block ever processed.

A cryptocurrency is a digital store of value primarily used to purchase and sell products, services, or property. Bitcoin and litecoin are two popular examples. These digital currencies are cryptographically safe against forgery and are frequently not issued or controlled by a centralized authority. Instead, the network's governance is left to the participants. Tokens and coins are other terms for cryptocurrency.

The difference is that blockchains have the potential to allow decentralized platforms that require a coin. The blockchain is a distributed ledger system that allows a network to maintain consensus. The network can track transactions and transfer value and information thanks to distributed consensus.

Tokens used within these networks to convey value and pay for transactions or offer network incentives are known as cryptocurrencies. Furthermore, they can be viewed as a blockchain tool, in some circumstances serving as a resource or service, or even to digitize asset ownership.

HOW BLOCKCHAIN MAKES CRYPTO ART AUTHENTIC

Recall that record that makes it simple to follow exchanges? That equivalent practice implies that a piece of computerized artistry can be followed as it trades hands and can be followed back to the first craftsman who made it. Its changing worth over the long run can likewise be followed. These variables are utilized to decide the general estimation of actual artistry pieces; however, recently, they were hard to follow in a computerized work that could be effortlessly shared or traced on the web.

HOW BLOCKCHAIN ADDS VALUE TO CRYPTO ART

Computerized craftsmanship is harder to claim than "customary" artistry. The issue of shareability again influences the work's worth. Blockchain permits craftsmanship authorities to possess computerized artistry in a new manner. Non-fungible tokens, or NFTs, are cryptographic tokens that are great snippets of data. It isn't for digital money in which 1 Bitcoin is equivalent to some other Bitcoin. One NFT addresses one novel piece of artistry. NFTs are additionally utilized for different things like possession records, computerized things, or space names. Along these lines, advanced specialists can sell their unique works and set up the worth to their pieces, which can be purchased by authorities who currently have a proprietorship record.

These reasons make crypto craftsmanship an energizing and genuinely novel thought. The truth will surface eventually if blockchain turns into a significant staple in advanced specialists' portfolios.

THE PRINCIPLE OF MINING

There's a reason why bitcoin mining is referred to as such. Solving mathematical puzzles to discover Bitcoins is quite similar to gold mining. Bitcoins, like gold, exist in a protocol's design and wait to be found, much as gold does for a long time before it is mined. So how does Bitcoin mining operate exactly?

When a Bitcoin owner transmits a legitimate transaction, it is added to the unconfirmed transactions to be processed. Each transaction includes an arbitrary charge for miners to earn as a reward for confirmation. The larger the cost, the more likely the transaction will be completed quickly. A certain number of transactions combine to form a block with a maximum size of 1MB. It is then up to each miner or pool to decide which transactions to include and how many to include in a block. The goal is to incorporate as many transactions as possible to acquire as many Bitcoins as feasible.

Following that, miners confirm the block by completing the allotted mathematical work - they must compute the correct hash that encrypts the block. The Bitcoin system establishes demands for what the hash should look like, and each miner competes to discover it first.

When the required hash is obtained, other miners confirm its validity, and the confirmed block of transactions is uploaded to the blockchain. A Blockchain is essentially a large account book that collects all Bitcoin transactions; it is transparent and allows you to track each Bitcoin movement.

❧ 2 ❧
UNDERSTANDING CRYPTO TOKEN

A crypto token is a virtual money token or a cryptocurrency denomination. It is a tradable asset or utility on its own blockchain and lets the holder utilize it for investment or economic objectives. Crypto tokens are another name for fungible tokens (or cryptotokens). These phrases are often reserved for fungible tokens other than the blockchain's principal cryptocurrency, that is, fungible tokens issued inside a smart contract operating on top of a blockchain like Ethereum.

Crypto tokens may be used to represent an investor's share in a firm or for economic purposes in the same way that legal money may. For example, this implies that token holders can use them to purchase items or trade them for profit, just like other securities.

HOW CRYPTO TOKEN WORK

A cryptocurrency token represents every traded item. This might be in the form of coins, points, certifications, in-game items, and so on. This indicates that crypto tokens might be used to represent shares in a corporation or voting rights on the central committee.

They are often used to generate revenue in crowd sales. As a result, they are also known as cryptocurrency assets, crypto assets, or crypto equity.

A digital token's creators may choose whether or not to put it on a cryptocurrency exchange. Users will be able to buy and sell the token in this way when the initial coin offering has concluded.

Tokens issued by the Ethereum Code may be frozen in the case of a hack or a government regulation. This means that no cryptocurrency tokens may be transferred until the freeze is lifted.

TYPES OF TOKENS

Tokens may look confusing at first glance. Bitcoin is the earliest and possibly most basic example of a digital token. It's variously referred to as digital currency or digital gold, but which is it? And what makes it valuable? And how exactly does it work? Going down this rabbit hole is entertaining, but it takes time and is ultimately unnecessary to get a high-level grasp of the many sorts of tokens.

Tokens include numerous complex differentiators, such as use case, structure, governance rights, fungibility, and others, and hence fall into several groups, similar to how taxonomies in biology are thought of. As a result, token designers are identifying and categorizing emergent tokens in the blockchain ecosystem in the same way that biologists categorized the globe into domains, kingdoms, phyla, and so on.

Tokens are classified into two types:

- Fungible
- Non-fungible.

FUNGIBLE TOKEN

Fungible tokens are virtually interchangeable and are often likened to dollar banknotes. You don't worry about the serial number or year of production on a dollar note given to you by a clerk since the one created in 1998 has the same nominal value and is accepted by the same people as the one created yesterday.

NON-FUNGIBLE TOKEN

Non-fungible tokens (NFTs) are distinct from one another. Plane tickets, for example, are one-of-a-kind in that they are associated with a certain person, time, flight, and destination. Thus, you can exchange plane tickets with anybody at the airport, but it's doubtful that you'll be able to use theirs to go to your intended location.

Fungible and Non-Fungible Usability

Fungible tokens are ideal for frequent transactions and standardized value swaps. For example, we intend Alice's bitcoin to be valued much like Bob's bitcoin and accepted by the same people. All Ethereum ERC-20 tokens, such as Augur or 0x, are likewise fungible, as are most other cryptocurrencies. You may use them to do the following:

- Deal with other people and businesses.
- Bet on certain outcomes (e.g., outcomes of an Augur prediction market)

- Stake in delivering a service (think taxi medallions)
- As collateral for cryptocurrency-backed loans
- Give out loans, as well as the majority of other things that money may be used for.

Non-fungible tokens often represented as ERC-721s on Ethereum, become much more intriguing since they may effectively represent anything in the world. These are divided into two categories: digitally native and digital representations. They may exist independently for the purpose of their existence or are linked to another item (whether physical or digital).

The most well-known example of a digitally native non-fungible token is Cryptokitties. They are a blockchain-based game that exists inside the Ethereum ecosystem. There were no real plushies on which the kittens were originally based, nor was there a prior version of the game that did not employ blockchain.

A popular example of a digital representation non-fungible token is land registries and homeownership "on the blockchain." But, of course, the land or house itself is not on the blockchain, but a record of it is. And if you establish non-fungible tokens on the blockchain that reflect land deeds so that whoever owns the token also owns the land, you've built a blockchain-based digital version of a real-world commodity.

CONSUMER TOKEN

This is another categorization that is critical to grasp, but designers are still ironing out the bugs. Consumer tokens are not a legally recognized distinction since nothing like it before existed, and it does not cleanly fit into any known precedent.

For the time being, consumer tokens are considered as providing access to a protocol's or company's goods or services without violating securities regulations.

When selling consumer tokens, projects should verify that consumers are purchasing and utilizing the token to engage with the protocol or company, not to speculate. This is beneficial for various reasons:

- If many speculators are holding the token, the price will be artificially high, making it difficult for normal people to participate with the protocol or firm.
- Speculators raise your token's volatility since they purchase and sell it based on its future price rather than its present use.
- Having genuine users, rather than speculators, own these tokens generates a community of individuals engaged with your product, offering feedback, recommending it to their friends, and overall assisting the network in growing.

Token Foundry recognizes this difference and has developed the Token Foundry Standards, a framework for selling consumer tokens and establishing decentralized networks so that the tokens offered for sale are directed to real users of these networks.

SECURITY TOKEN

On the other hand, security tokens are tradable blockchain-based assets that meet the standard of securities under conventional standards (i.e., debt or equity). Therefore, they are subject to the same rules as traditional non-blockchain-based securities. There are two particularly promising areas in the world of security tokens:

- More things are becoming securitized.
- Increasing security, execution speed, efficiency, and liquidity.

The practice of "converting (an asset, particularly a loan) into marketable securities, often for the aim of generating cash by selling them to other investors" is known as securitization. There are significant legal and financial constraints and restrictions and third-party costs involved in the issue, management, tracking, securing, trading execution, settlement, and so on of these securities.

Blockchain and, more especially, smart contracts have the potential to reduce those costs while also increasing the liquidity of these securities, eliminating intermediaries to boost efficiency and speed of execution, and making them safer (code is law). Many hitherto unattainable assets, such as fine art, might be securitized, allowing for partial ownership. You might also establish auditable collateralized debt obligations with programmatically specified payments to owners of different tranches that auto-execute, removing tremendous inefficiencies in reconciliation.

The fascinating part is that fungible versus non-fungible classifications and consumer versus security classifications really interact. You can have:

- Augur tokens, for example, are fungible consumer tokens.
- Consumer tokens that are not fungible, such as Cryptokitties
- Fungible securities, such as blockchain-based stocks
- Securities that are not fungible, such as blockchain-based property titles

Aside from the categories we've previously identified, the fact is that we're more interested in the ones that are still a mystery. Nobody could have imagined the internet's remarkable achievements and how they would completely disrupt our social structures, networks, work methods, and many other things. This is the power of tokens right now - we don't know what will happen, but we know it will be fantastic.

❦ 3 ❦
WHAT ARE ETHEREUM TOKENS?

Ethereum is a blockchain-based decentralized platform built for smart contract execution. A smart contract is a program that executes precisely as its developer programmed it. It is simply an execution that may be pre-programmed to run automatically when specific criteria have been met.

The Ethereum Virtual Machine (EVM) operates on the Ethereum network and enables anybody to execute a program, greatly simplifying the process of developing blockchain applications. Developers do not need to create a new blockchain from the start for each application, nor are they restricted to a single programming language.

In essence, Ethereum is constructing the first public blockchain-based decentralized global computer.

Smart contracts are significant because they enable the development of decentralized apps (dApps) that may automate tasks and function without censorship or downtime.

As you are aware, Ethereum's native currency is called Ether (ETH), and it is used to run the network via transaction fees. However, one of Ethereum's most essential features is the potential for anybody to create unique tokens that exist and run on the Ethereum blockchain — tokens that may serve various utility-like functions.

THE ERC STANDARD

ERC is an abbreviation for Ethereum Request for Comments. ERCs are Ethereum application-level standards containing token standards, name registries, library/package formats, and other features. Anyone may build an ERC, but the author must adequately describe their standard and encourage community acceptance for it.

Common ERC standards specify a set of needed functionalities for a token type, enabling applications and smart contracts to communicate with them predictably.

To date, the most commonly used ERC standard is the ERC-20, a sort of standard that simplifies the development, usage, and exchange of Ethereum-based tokens.

On the other hand, crypto enthusiasts should be mindful of the challenges that may develop when different projects accept restricted functionality from each standard, causing their smart contracts to diverge from a true ERC standard. This is a topic we'll go into in the last section of this chapter. For the time being, let us focus on the many types of ERC standards.

DIFFERENT KINDS OF ERCS

Many ERC standards perform various functions. However, the following are the top five in terms of adoption and usability:

- **ERC-20:** This is the standard API for fungible tokens, which includes transfer and balance monitoring features.
- **ERC-223:** This standard safeguards users against unintentional contract transfers.
- **ERC-721** is the most widely used non-fungible token (NFT) standard. Non-fungible tokens cannot be split, but fungible tokens may. Individuals may own and trade NFTs, as well as assign them to other parties. NFTs may denote ownership of either digital or physical assets.
- **ERC-809:** This protocol is used to rent out competing non-fungible tokens. An NFT is regarded as a 'rival' if its use/ownership by one person precludes other people from using/owning it at the same time. ERC-809 enables an owner to rent access to competing NFTs using a common set of instructions, and users may examine all previous and present rental agreements through a single wallet interface.
- **ERC-1238:** This standard applies to non-transferable tokens (sometimes known as "badges").

THE ADVANTAGES AND DISADVANTAGES OF ERCS

There are several advantages of utilizing ERC standards. They, like libraries, assist developers in using proven code rather than constructing from scratch. They also allow users to deploy code for standard-like operations more quickly. Token contracts, crowdsales (popular during the ICO boom), escrows, and tracking are a few examples.

With ERCs, it is simple to develop wizards and oracles on top of smart contract apps to provide improved user interfaces.

The issue is that certain ERC contracts, particularly those deployed during the ICO boom, do not completely adhere to the rules.

Although it may seem that the implications are little, this is not the case. For example, if another development team wants to utilize a certain token verified as an ERC-20 on a smart contract application they have created, but the smart contract does not completely adhere to the ERC-20 standard, the token may be lost due to a lack of functionality.

As a result, if a smart contract is considered an ERC-20, it should include complete ERC-20 capability; otherwise, developer errors may occur. Another problem – and this is a significant one – is that certain smart contracts may not ensure that a certain asset is entirely in the user's control.

❧ 4 ❧

THE NON-FUNGIBLE TOKENS
(NFTS)

B efore delving into the complexities of NFTs, it's important to understand the distinction between "fungible" and "non-fungible." For all intents and purposes, a fungible object or token is interchangeable with another unit of the same thing.

One Bitcoin, for example, is comparable to another Bitcoin, just as one US dollar is equivalent to another US dollar. So if you give a buddy a $10 note, they do not have to return the loan with the same $10 note; any $10 note would suffice.

Non-fungible things, on the other hand, are not interchangeable and contain distinct features that might make them fundamentally different from one another, even though they seem identical.

In the actual world, there are several instances of nonfungible items, such as paintings, concert tickets, and so on. For example, although two paintings may seem to be the same, their rarity levels may be vastly different. Similarly, front row tickets to a show are much more valuable than back row tickets.

CAMERON BELFORD

WHAT ARE NON-FUNGIBLE TOKENS?

This takes us to the topic of non-fungible tokens (NFTs). What exactly are they, and how do they differ from non-fungible digital assets such as domain names or Twitter handles? Non-fungible tokens are a kind of token that provides a flexible mechanism to represent non-fungible assets on a blockchain. It is a digital asset that signifies real-word objects such as art, music, in-game goods, and films. They are purchased and traded online, usually using cryptocurrency, and are often encoded using the same underlying software as many cryptos.

Even though they have been present since 2014, NFTs are gaining popularity as a popular means to purchase and sell digital artwork. Since November 2017, a whopping $174 million has been spent on NFTs.

NFTs are also often one-of-a-kind, or at the very least one of a very limited run, with unique identification codes. "Essentially, NFTs generate digital scarcity," explains Arry Yu, managing director of Yellow Umbrella Ventures and head of the Washington Technology Industry Association Cascadia Blockchain Council.

This is in sharp contrast to the vast majority of digital creations, which are virtually endless in quantity. Therefore, cutting down supply should theoretically increase the value of a particular item if it is in demand.

However, many NFTs, at least in the beginning, were digital works that already existed in some form elsewhere, such as memorable video clips from NBA games or securitized copies of digital art that were already circulating on Instagram.

For example, famed digital artist Mike Winklemann, better known as "Beeple," produced a composite of 5,000 daily drawings to produce possibly the most renowned NFT of the time, "EVERYDAYS: The First 5000 Days," which sold for a record-breaking $69.3 million at Christie's.

Individual images—or perhaps the full collage of images—can be seen online for free by anybody. So why are individuals prepared to pay millions of dollars on something that they can simply capture or download?

Because an NFT permits the buyer to retain ownership of the original item, it has built-in authentication, which acts as evidence of ownership. Collectors appreciate "digital bragging rights" nearly as much as the thing itself.

Non-fungible tokens primary characteristics are as follows:

- **Uncommon**: Non-fungible tokens have information in their code that explains the attributes of each token that distinguishes it from others. A piece of digital art may have coded information on individual pixels, while tokenized in-game things may include information that allows the game client to determine which object the player owns and its properties.
- **Traceability**: Each NFT records transactions on-chain dating back to when it was created, including each time it changed hands. This implies that each token can be verified as legitimate and not a forgery - clearly a critical factor for owners and potential buyers!
- **Rare**: Non-fungible tokens should be provably rare to be appealing to purchasers. This ensures that assets stay attractive in the long term and

that supply does not exceed demand.

Indivisible: Most NFTs cannot be traded in fractions of a whole. Non-fungible tokens cannot be divided into smaller values in the same way that a concert ticket or trading card cannot be purchased in half.

- **Programmability**: NFTs, like other conventional digital assets and tokens based on smart contract blockchains, are completely programmable. Breeding mechanisms are included directly in the coins of CryptoKitties and Axie Infinity. It is possible to add much more features.

In other words, non-fungible assets are combined with the finest features of decentralized blockchain technology. Unlike traditional digital assets issued and governed by centralized bodies and may be taken away at any moment, you may own and manage your own NFTs.

DIFFERENCE BETWEEN NON-FUNGIBLE TOKENS AND CRYPTOCURRENCY

NFT is an abbreviation for non-fungible tokens. It is often created with the same programming as cryptocurrencies such as Bitcoin or Ethereum, but that is where the similarities stop.

Physical currency and cryptocurrencies are both "fungible," which means they may be traded or swapped for one another. They're also worth the same—one dollar is always worth another dollar, and one Bitcoin is always worth another Bitcoin. The fungibility of cryptocurrency gives it a reliable method of executing blockchain transactions.

NFTs are distinct. Each has a digital signature, which prohibits NFTs from being substituted for or equal to one another (hence, non-fungible). Because they're both NFTs, one NBA Top Shot clip isn't the same as EVERYDAYS. (For that matter, one NBA Top Shot clip is not necessarily comparable to another NBA Top Shot clip.)

NON-FUNGIBLE TOKEN EXAMPLES

NFT stand for something distinct, something that is not transferable. The CRYPTOPUNKS project provided the first example of Non-Fungible Tokens. Users were able to sell, purchase, and keep 10,000 distinct collectible characters, with evidence of ownership recorded on the Ethereum Blockchain.

Decentralized Art and Collections

Because the value of art is determined by various characteristics such as authenticity, age, and the number of owners, storing it as an NFT on the blockchain makes perfect sense.

Artists often struggle to prove the authenticity of their work, particularly in the case of digital art. However, the introduction of Blockchain and NFTs may aid in the resolution of this issue. Currently, an artist may post their artwork on their website, social media, or a blogging site, but this does not show ownership, and many of these sites do not even provide a legitimate date stamp.

However, by using Blockchain and NFTs, artists may submit their artwork to a website, which adds them to the blockchain. This implies that the author's information and the artwork's legitimacy may be kept on the tamperproof and secure blockchain. Furthermore, because everything is documented on a public ledger, it is feasible to trace the art back to its original owner and the day it was released.

1. KnownOrigin

KnownOrigin is a forum where artists can display and sell their unique digital artwork and collectibles. Buying art used to be exceedingly difficult for ordinary people due to the difficulty of verifying authenticity without the assistance of art professional. On the other hand, users can quickly identify the genuine owner and have trust in their purchase by using KnownOrigin.

The platform uses the Ethereum network, enabling artists to tokenize their work and then list it as a unique NFT on the KnownOrigin website. When a piece of art is purchased using ETH, the buyer's address is recorded. This permits the new author's identity to be registered on the blockchain.

Since its start in 2018, the digital art platform has hosted over 1000 artists and sold over 17,000 pieces of art. The BlockRocket team created the website.

2. Bitcoin Origins

Bitcoin Origins is a limited-edition collection of digital collectible cards that commemorate the most pivotal milestones in Bitcoin's history. The cards are all designed by outstanding artists and are available on the Bitcoin Origins website, where they sell out in seconds on the WAX Blockchain.

3. Cryptograph

Many people in the Blockchain community have recently learned that Paris Hilton sold her digital artwork of a cat for 40 ETH, which equated to a stunning $17,000 at the time of sale. This was made possible with the assistance of the charity digital art website Cryptograph.

Cryptograph enables users to sell collectibles, which are often renowned drawings, schematics, or paintings. These collectibles are often manufactured by celebrities such as Paris Hilton, Seth Green, and Ashley Greene. All of these celebrities have put their art up for sale on the website using ETH.

The platform was created primarily to generate funds for charity organizations, and it has raised thousands of dollars since its start.

NFT Games

Non-Fungible Tokens have also made it possible for gaming and blockchain to collaborate. NFTs are one-of-a-kind, which is major news in the gaming industry. This is because being unique implies that something is scarce, making it valuable to other players. Because of the competitive nature of games, players are always striving to create a better character, world or get better add-ons or benefits.

4. Sorare

Sorare is a fantasy football trading card game in which users may trade the cards of actual players and manage their teams to win enormous weekly rewards. There are presently 126 approved clubs in the fantasy football game, including teams from major leagues such as the Premier League, Bundesliga, Serie A, and European championships like the Champions League.

Every week, Sorare conducts various tournaments (So5) in which players may join their teams (of 5 players) and compete for rewards. Prizes range from 0.01 ETH to tradable cards valued at millions of dollars.

All of the cards are NFTs, and they are all kept on the Ethereum Blockchain. Because all of the information is kept in the asset's meta description, the ownership of the cards can be confirmed. Furthermore, because everything is maintained on a public ledger, everyone on the platform can observe all of the platform's transactions.

5. NBA Top Shot

NBA Top Shot has swiftly become one of the largest growing NFT projects, operating on top of the Flow Blockchain, which also manages several significant licensed NFT applications such as MotoGP Ignition and the impending Dr. Seuss.

NBA Top Shot Moments is a collection of collectible trading cards based on National Basketball Association (NBA) players. In actuality, the trade cards include more than simply an image and basic data about each player, with a short video, generally of their finest performance in a game, also included.

The players are published in various "sets," which are generally highly styled and centered on a certain theme, such as "MVP Moves" and "Conference Semifinals." Within these packs, players are granted rarities, which then decide how many editions of that "Moment" have been generated.

6. Crypto Kitties

Crypto Kitties is a game that enables players to trade virtual cats known as "Crypto Kitties," allowing them to buy and sell cats, play games, and construct collections to receive prizes.

According to the game, "each cat is one-of-a-kind and completely yours; it cannot be reproduced, taken away, or killed." Because of the nature of Blockchain and NFTs, this is conceivable. Due to the resilient structure of the blockchain, elements/blocks cannot be easily deleted since they are linked to other blocks in a chain.

Because Virtual Cats are NFTs, they have information contained in their meta description that includes facts such as the asset's owner and what makes it special.

The game was so popular in 2017 that it caused transactions on the Ethereum network to slow down, resulting in a six-fold increase in pending transactions. This exposed some of Ethereum's scalability concerns, which is one of the reasons Etheruem is currently considering converting to Proof of Stake.

Domain naming services

There is presently a great deal of centralization in domains and the internet as a whole. For example, we pay the companies that own.com and.net names only to have the right to rent their names. Due to the centralization, large websites such as TikTok are also being restricted throughout the globe.

Because of their centralized nature, these domains and systems are often susceptible to hacking; all domain ownership information is stored on these centralized servers. However, because there is no centralized location to attack when this information is kept on the blockchain, the system becomes far more resilient and safe.

7. Handshake Domains

Handshake is a naming and certificate authority that is decentralized. It confirms domain ownership without the necessity for a central authority to have control over them. This ensures that your website's domain will never be blocked.

Domains purchased from NameBase.io are then held on the HandShake Blockchain. This implies that the buyer's information may be kept on the blockchain without requiring a centralized entity to do so.

The initiative has received more than $10 million in investment from enthusiastic investors who see the advantages of a decentralized web.

HOW NON-FUNGIBLE TOKEN WORKS

NFTs are stored on a blockchain, which is a distributed public ledger that records transactions. You've heard of blockchain as the fundamental technique that allows cryptocurrencies to exist.

NFTs are commonly kept on the Ethereum blockchain; however, they may also be kept on other blockchains.

An NFT is formed, or "minted," using digital objects

representing both physical and intangible elements, such as:

- Music
- Designer sneakers
- Virtual avatars and video game skins
- Collectibles
- Videos and sports highlights
- GIFs
- Art

Tweets are also counted. Jack Dorsey, the co-founder of Twitter, sold his first tweet as an NFT for more than $2.9 million.

NFTs are essentially digital collector's items, similar to actual collector's items. However, instead of receiving a physical oil painting to put on the wall, the customer receives a digital file.

They will also have exclusive ownership rights. That's correct: NFTs can only have one owner at a time. The unique data of NFTs makes it simple to verify ownership and transfer tokens between owners. They may also be used to hold particular information by the owner or author. Artists, for example, may sign their work by putting their signature in the metadata of an NFT.

NFT USABILITY

Blockchain technology and NFTs provide artists and content creators with a one-of-a-kind possibility to monetize their work. Artists, for example, no longer have to depend on galleries or auction houses to sell their work. Instead, the artist may sell it straight to the buyer as an

NFT, allowing them to retain a larger portion of the revenues. Furthermore, artists may automate royalties to get a proportion of revenues anytime their artwork is sold to a new owner. This is an appealing feature since most artists do not earn future revenue once their work is sold.

Art isn't the only method to profit from NFTs. Charmin and Taco Bell, for example, have auctioned off themed NFT paintings to generate revenue for charity. Charmin's offering was called "NFTP" (non-fungible toilet paper), while Taco Bell's NFT art sold out in minutes, with the top bids coming in at 1.5 wrapped ether (WETH)—equivalent to $3,723.83 at the time of writing.

Nyan Cat, a 2011 GIF depicting a cat with a pop-tart body, sold for more than $600,000 in February 2021. As of late March, NBA Top Shot had sold more than $500 million. A single LeBron James highlight NFT sold for more than $200,000.

Celebrities such as Snoop Dogg and Lindsay Lohan have jumped on the NFT bandwagon, releasing securitized memories, artwork, and experiences as securitized NFTs.

HISTORY OF NON-FUNGIBLE TOKEN (NFT)

Non-fungible tokens have been around for a lot longer than you would believe. Following the creation of Bitcoin in 2009 and the subsequent proliferation of token types such as Litecoin, Ripple, and others, many individuals sought to develop on blockchain technology to build newer, more powerful tokens. This section will provide you with a short history of NFTs.

COLORED COINS

Colored coins, which were initially proposed in a blog post by Yoni Assia in March 2012, were probably the first forerunners of non-fungible tokens. These were extremely tiny Bitcoin units that had unique features programmed into metadata using Bitcoin's scripting language. As a result, units as small as one satoshi (0.00000001 BTC) might represent any asset imaginable, such as a dollar, stock in a firm, a house, or digital collectibles.

Although the idea of colored coins seemed to be highly

intriguing and potentially powerful, it had many problems and roadblocks:

1. Colored coins were not officially supported by the Bitcoin network. As a result, it was up to wallet providers to detect the presence of colored coins.

2. Back then, the minimum transaction size for a Bitcoin transaction was adjusted to 5,430 satoshis (0.000543 BTC), which was much too huge to deploy colored coins.

3. Colored coins enabled the development of any asset, not simply NFTs. Since a result, the advent of Ethereum's ERC-20 token standard in 2015 removed much of the usefulness of colored coins, as ERC-20 is much more versatile. Meanwhile, platforms like Counterparty have taken over the NFT function of colored coins.

As a result, colored coins gradually fizzled and went away. Coinprism, the first wallet to allow colored currencies, stopped down in 2018, citing legal pressure as well as the Bitcoin network's inflexibility and relative sluggishness.

COUNTERPARTY.IO

Counterparty was formed in 2014 to issue non-fungible and semi-fungible tokens based on the concept of colored currencies. Counterparty's creators saw that Bitcoin lacked the characteristics required to build a sophisticated asset creation and trading platform.

The mobile game Spells of Genesis was the first to

release in-game assets onto any blockchain in 2015, using Counterparty. In 2016, the popular trading card game Force of Will launched cards on Counterparty, extending the platform's success. Force of Will was the fourth most popular trading card game in North America at the time, behind household names like Magic: The Gathering, Poké-mon, and Yu-Gi-Oh.

Although blockchain-based in-game assets will continue to be used, the most significant innovation occurred in 2016, when users started producing limited edition Rare Pepes on Counterparty based on the popular and often contentious meme figure Pepe the Frog. Of course, the concept of a "unique" internet image is nonsensical since they are readily replicated, but people have been debating it since 2015.

Although you could view Rare Pepe cards as frivolous, they serve as striking evidence of the human urge to acquire anything that is both rare and has some widely recognized aesthetic or collector value, a combination that enabled Rare Pepes to become an immediate hit. As a result, rare Pepes may fetch thousands of dollars, with the peak being a historic digital art auction in 2019, when an ultra-rare, one-of-a-kind Homer Simpson Pepe fetched $38,500.

CRYPTOPUNKS

With the success of Rare Pepes as a model, John Watkinson and Matt Hall produced CryptoPunks in June 2017 — algorithmically produced, 24x24 pixel characters that reside on the Ethereum blockchain. Unfortunately, only 10,000 characters with distinct looks were produced. The CryptoPunks creators made it possible for anybody to claim the Punks for free — unsurprisingly, all 10,000 were swiftly taken.

Although CryptoPunks were already a viral hit when they were originally released, they have recently piqued the interest of the NFT community. As the first "true NFT" to debut on Ethereum, many people use Punk ownership as a badge of honor, almost as a status symbol proving that the owner is a "true OG" of the crypto world. CryptoPunks realized prices had soared to thousands of dollars in the last three months.

Because CryptoPunks was founded before the ERC-721 non-fungible token standard, the founders were forced to use a modified ERC-20 token for the Punks (token address). Nonetheless, CryptoPunks inspired the ERC-721 standard, paving the path for the next genuinely viral NFT sensation: CryptoKitties.

CRYPTOKITTIES

CryptoKitties was established in October of 2017. It was a virtual game in which players could breed, nurture, and sell virtual cats with distinct genomes that influenced their looks. CryptoKitties, which were released in the middle of the late 2017 crypto craze, quickly rose in value, with one CryptoKitty buying 600 ETH (US$172k at the time). The initiative was covered extensively in the mainstream media, including CNN, CNBC, and the Financial Times.

Today, CryptoKitties activity has slowed slightly, with the project ranking 13th in terms of volume traded over the last week, according to NonFungible.com. However, we cannot overstate the project's impact on the NFT landscape – the project is still ranked first in terms of all-time volume traded, with over $38 million worth of CryptoKitties transacted since 2017.

TOP NFT PROJECTS

Many initiatives have sprouted up in NFTs since 2017. According to The Block Research, there are now at least 73 NFT platforms — Below are some of the more notable ones:

- CryptoPunks: CryptoPunks are collectible characters that were developed algorithmically.
- Avatars: Avatars may be minted and collected by users.
- Meme: Farming tokens that may be redeemed for limited edition collectible NFTs.
- Axie Infinity: Gather, nurture, and breed Axies for use in combat.
- CryptoKitties: Buy, breed, trade, and collect one-of-a-kind digital kitties.
- Sorare is a fantasy football game in which players acquire, trade, and field player cards.
- Decentraland: An Ethereum-based virtual world where users may exchange virtual real estate.
- Cryptovoxels: In this virtual world, you may buy property, create businesses and art galleries, and conduct events.
- Ethereum Name Service: Register a named. eth domain to accept payments.
- Unstoppable Domains: a platform that allows you to register blockchain domains for your cryptocurrency wallets.
- SuperRare is a digital art marketplace.

- Rarible is a digital collectibles marketplace. To farm RARI token, trade on Rarible.
- OpenSea is a peer-to-peer marketplace for all NFTs.
- Aavegotchi: Own and sell avatars backed by interest-bearing tokens representing loans on Defi lending platform Aave.
- NFTfi: Use NFTs as loan collateral.

❦ 6 ❧

ADVANTAGES AND DISADVANTAGES OF NON-FUNGIBLE TOKENS

Presently, NFTs have their advantages and disadvantages like any innovation, and in this segment, the accompanying can be featured.

NFTS ADVANTAGES

- They permit us to address computerized and genuine items in an interesting and unrepeatable manner inside the blockchain. So we can utilize this innovation to deal with these articles securely and consistently. Would you like to tokenize your home or your vehicle utilizing NFT? You can do it. Your creative mind is the cutoff.

- The advancement prospects of NFTs are perpetual; anything that you can address carefully can turn into an NFT. For instance, space names (those used to distinguish website pages) can be addressed as an NFT inside a

DNS on the BlockchainBlockchain. This is the thing that occurs with the Namecoin project and the Ethereum Name Service.

- The production of NFT can be adjusted to any blockchain, and it tends to be executed in an extremely secure manner. A model is Bitcoin, which with its restricted programming limit, can address NFTs, keeping the security hazards for such resources for a base; it figures out how to address NFTs.
- The presence of norms makes their creation, execution, and advancement simpler.
- Opportunities for cross-chain interoperability with tasks like Polkadot or Cosmos.

NFTS DISADVANTAGES

- While there are norms for creating NFT, they are neither dependable nor complete as far as usefulness is concerned. The previously mentioned is the primary motivation behind why, for instance, the ERC-721 badge of Ethereum (the most utilized for NFT in Ethereum) tries to be supplanted by the ERC-1155 token significantly more secure and has new capacities.
- NFTs are overseen by complex shrewd agreements, making their tasks mind-blogging and weighty (as far as data). These two things raise the estimation of the commissions that should be paid to complete exchanges. So,

running NFT can be costly, particularly if the organization is blocked and commissions soar.

- Like Defi, NFT stages are more defenseless to hacks since everything is taken care of by brilliant agreements and different interfaces to control them. This whole layer of programming adds assault vectors that programmers can misuse for malignant increase.

NON-FUNGIBLE TOKENS VALUE

NFTs derive their value from the same deflationary principles as bitcoin—the number of tokens is limited, and the articles cannot be replicated. Authenticity also plays a role in the verified and can always be traced back to the original creator. Thus, owners of NFT tokens can fully own these individual digital assets knowing that they own only such tokens.

The value of NFTs is also based on the immutability of the product. NFTs cannot be destroyed, deleted, or duplicated. The token only exists on its native platform. It is stored on the blockchain items from one platform and cannot be moved to another.

The Nonfungible.com website found that the number of NFT buyers increased by 66% in 2020, while the value of transactions rose from around $63 million to $250 million (52 to 207 million euros).

Non-fungible tokens are unified and extraordinary crypto resources that help make computerized shortages. NFTs have been made on the Ethereum (ETH) blockchain, as per the ERC-721 norm. Today, in any case, they are accessible on numerous other blockchains, similar to EOS, TRON, and NEO, and have many use cases. For example, NFTs can address advanced collectibles, crafts-manship, or in-game resources.

NFTs and their smart contracts contain distinguishing data, which makes each NFT special. Thus, no two NFTs are similar. For instance, you can trade one ticket for one more of a similar section on the account of banknotes. They have equal worth, so it doesn't make any difference which one you own.

Bitcoin (BTC) is a convertible token. You can send 1 BTC to somebody; at that point, they can move it else-where. However, its worth is as yet equivalent to one bitcoin. Since convertible digital currencies are separable, you can likewise send or get a more modest part of bitcoin-satoshi.

One of the primary NFT collectibles was Cryptokit-ties, an Ethereum blockchain-based game that permits clients to gather and raise virtual felines. Each blockchain-based talk is interesting.

MOST EXPENSIVE NON-FUNGIBLE TOKENS
EVER SOLD

1. Beeple, Everydays (The First 5000 Days, $69 million)

Beeple takes the top spot in our ranking, thanks to the most remarkable and surprising sale of this period. Christie's closes his first online auction on March 11th, in which he has a work NFT that soars from an initial evalua-tion of $100 to a record of $69 million in a very short period. Beeple, therefore, found himself the third living artist most expensive in the world behind himself in Jeff Koons and David Hockney.

2. Virtual Images of Rick and Morty ($2.3 million)

Another craftsman who has figured out how to sell show-stoppers as NFT at an over-the-top cost is Justin Roiland, the maker of the famous energized arrangement "Rick and Morty." His assortment of 16 masterpieces was sold for 1,300 ETH, which was near $2.3 million.

A part of the closeout returns was dispensed to assisting the needy with peopling in Los Angeles, with Roiland saying it was an approach to test the restrictions of crypto artistry.

Strangely, a portion of Roiland's work of art has been delivered in numerous duplicates. Works named "It's Tree Guy" and "Qualified Bachelors" cost $10 and $100 for each piece, separately.

Show-stoppers made in a solitary duplicate were sold at greater costs because of their uniqueness and extraordinariness. The play called "The Simpsons" sold for $290,100. The closeout's beginning cost was $14,999, with its actual being sold for a similar sum.

3. Land on Axie Infinity ($1.5 million)

In the first and second positions, we put computerized craftsmanship assortments that were sold through different exchanges. This time, nine land plots on the well-known blockchain game Axie Infinity were sold in a solitary NFT exchange. The client who made the buy paid 888.5 ETH, or $1.5 million, at that point.

Axie Infinity permits clients to construct a realm in which fabulous characteristics live. The existence where you can purchase virtual land is called Lunacia and has a set number of spots. The entire plot is separated into 90,601 more modest plots, 19,601 more modest plots, 19% of which are possessed by players.

Hawk called attention that the land he purchased is in a great area. Moreover, the pattern on Axie Infinity is consistently expanding, as confirmed by the developing number of dynamic clients. Later on, it will likewise be feasible to arrange occasions, like celebrations or shows, on "your territory" and accordingly bring in cash.

4. Collectible character on CryptoPunks ($762,000)

Toward the finish of January, an NFT portraying a character from the CryptoPunks game was sold for 605 ETH, or $762,000, at that point. The universe of Crypto-Punks is enlivened by crypto artistry development and comprises more than 10,000 extraordinary advanced characters.

Today, they can be purchased and sold in the committed CyberPunks market. It ought to be referenced that already the characters in the game were free, and you simply expected to have an ETH wallet to get them.

The NFT, which was initially found in 2017 and sold at an exorbitant cost, is $2,890. It is a very uncommon 'punk.'

5. A visit to the blockchain game CryptoKitties (600 ETH)

The following most costly NFT in history is Dragon from the blockchain game CryptoKitties. This adorable advanced feline was sold for 600 ETH, or $200,000, at that point. Today, a similar measure of tokens costs around $1,000,000 million.

CryptoKitties is one of the main endeavors to utilize blockchain innovation for diversion. The Axiom Zen studio created it. Like real felines, each virtual feline has a special DNA and its qualities called "credits," which can be given to posterity. Furthermore, each virtual feline is one of a kind and can't be repeated or moved without the proprietor's permission.

As a rule, past ages of virtual felines are viewed as more important. Dragon uncommon—this is the 10th era of CrytoKitty.

6. A Delta Time F1 vehicle ($110,000)

Another NFT is a Formula 1 vehicle on the F1 Delta Time game, explicitly the 1-1-1 model. An unknown gamer purchased this dashing virtual vehicle for an amazing measure of 415.5 ETH. At the hour of procurement, it was more than $110,000. Until now, such a measure of ETH is worth around $665,000. This buy got the title of the greatest NFT exchange in 2019.

7. One F1 Delta Time track ($200,000)

This time, nonetheless, not a vehicle but rather part of a track. Toward the beginning of December 2020, a piece of track on F1 Delta Time was sold for more than 9,000,000 REVV tokens, or $200,000, at that point. From that point forward, EVV has developed by 500%, and at the hour of composing this book, it would cost $1.2 million for a similar measure of REVV.

For F1 Delta Time, all significant game resources are addressed by NFTs. For example, the Circuit de Monaco's virtual track comprises 330 badges of this kind partitioned into four levels—from "Uncommon" to Summit." Each token addresses a virtual track share, giving its proprietor a bunch of advantages.

For this specific NFT, it was at the "Zenith" level. As a result, its purchaser will get 5% of all in-game income and 4.2% of first-class marking benefits from player stores. Both will be paid in REVV utility tokens.

8. NFT Guarantee Money Insurance (350 ETH)

"5000.0 ETH-Cover-NFT" is a protection strategy

dependent on yinsure. Money, an undertaking upheld by Yearn. Financial Because of an enthusiastic advanced approach, its proprietor profits by protection against mistakes in keen agreements on Curve.fi up to 5,000 ETH. NFT costs 350 ETH, which compares to more than $560,000 today.

Yinsure is otherwise called Cover, So, it is a consolidated protection inclusion ensured by Nexus Mutual and another sort of tokenized protection. Protection approaches are represented as NFT. Every one of them is a special NFT. Otherwise called NFT, and can be moved, purchased, or sold.

9. 12,600 square meters of virtual land in Decentraland (514 ETH)

Somebody purchased 12,600 m2 for 514 ETH on the Decentraland blockchain game. The game is an Ethereum-based decentralized augmented experience stage. Its clients can make, analyze, and adapt their substance and applications.

Decentraland has a restricted 3D virtual space called LAND. It is a non-fungible computerized resource kept up by Ethereum shrewd agreements. The landowner has full control of their virtual land.

10. Land at 22.2 in Decentraland (345 ETH)

Here is Decentraland once more. This time, it's a land parcel in a "great area" at 22.2. In the realm of Decentraland, the size of the land is fixed. About 80% of its space is private, and the vast majority of the rest is sold and rented by Decentraland. The excess land, like streets and squares, doesn't have a place with anybody. Players can just walk their characters on their territory and public land, so the situation is very significant. Parts found nearer to well-known regions will be more costly than those situated in more distant zones.

Taking a gander at how quickly the NFT markets are developing and what costs non-fungible tokens are sold, we can accept that this will be another gigantic pattern just after Defi. A significant quality of NFTs is that each has its own remarkable and interesting attributes.

ৠ 7 ৠ

STEP-BY-STEP GUIDE TO NFT TRADING

NFTs have quickly become one of the biggest crypto fads of 2021, with total sales increasing by 55 percent from 2020, from $250 million to $389 million. This chapter will examine how to make, buy, and trade these popular digital assets in a step-by-step procedure.

Non-fungible tokens (NFTs), which are collectible crypto assets, have existed since the notion of Bitcoin Colored Coins first surfaced in 2012. These coins were simply satoshis – small fractions of a bitcoin – marked, or "colored in," with distinct information that could link the coins to real-world assets, such as "this satoshi represents $500 of John Doe's New York office building." Colored Coins were mostly used to create and trade artwork like "Rare Pepe" digital cards on Counterparty, a peer-to-peer trading platform.

These cartoon frog graphics were among the first instances of one-of-a-kind digital artwork linked to cryptocurrency tokens based on a big internet meme. This cleared the door for creating and developing new non-fungible token standards — a collection of blockchain building blocks that let developers design their own NFTs.

NFTs may represent almost any form of physical or immaterial thing, including:

- Artwork
- Skins, virtual cash, weapons, and avatars are examples of virtual items found in video games.
- Music
- Collectibles (e.g., digital trading cards)
- Real-world assets that have been tokenized range from real estate and automobiles to racehorses and designer sneakers.
- Land in the virtual realm
- Video footage of iconic sporting moments

STEP-BY-STEP GUIDE TO MAKING NON-FUNGIBLE TOKEN (NFT)

Creating your own NFT artwork, whether in the form of a GIF or an image, is a reasonably simple procedure that does not need a considerable understanding of the crypto sector. NFT artwork may also be utilized to make collectibles such as digital card sets.

Step 1

Before you begin, you must determine on which blockchain you wish to issue your NFTs on. Ethereum is now the most popular blockchain service for issuing NFTs. However, various alternative blockchains are gaining popularity, including WAX, Cosmos, Tezos, EOS,

Polkadot, Tron, Flow by Dapper Labs, Binance Smart Chain.

Every blockchain has its own NFT token standard as well as wallet services and marketplaces. For example, if you build NFTs on top of the Binance Smart Chain, you can only sell them on sites that accept Binance Smart Chain assets. Unfortunately, this means you won't be able to sell them on platforms like VIV3, a Flow blockchain-based marketplace, or OpenSea, an Ethereum-based NFT marketplace.

Step 2

Because Ethereum has the biggest NFT ecosystem, you'll need the following to mint your own NFT artwork, music, or video on the Ethereum blockchain:

MetaMask, Trust Wallet, or Coinbase Wallet are examples of Ethereum wallets that support ERC-721 (the Ethereum-based NFT token standard).

Approximately $50-$100 in ether (ETH). If you use Coinbase's wallet, you may purchase ether using US dollars, British pounds sterling, and other fiat currencies. You'll have to buy ether from a cryptocurrency exchange otherwise.

Step 3

Once you have them, you can link your wallet to various NFT-centric services and upload the picture or file you wish to make into an NFT.

The most popular Ethereum NFT exchanges are:

- Mintable

- Rarible
- OpenSea

You can also make your own NFTs on Makersplace, but you must first register as a listed artist on the site.

Step 4

In the upper right corner of OpenSea, Rarible, and Mintable, there is a "create" button. OpenSea, is one of the world's biggest Ethereum-based NFT marketplaces; this is how it works:

Step 5

When you click the blue "Create" button, you'll be taken to a page where you'll be asked to link your Ethereum wallet. When you provide your wallet password when prompted, your wallet will be instantly connected to the marketplace. To confirm you hold the wallet address, you may need to digitally sign a message in your Ethereum wallet, but it's only a matter of clicking through.

There is no charge for digitally signing a message; it is just a way to demonstrate that you own the wallet.

Step 6

On OpenSea, navigate to "create" in the upper right corner and pick "my collections." Then click the blue "create" button.

Step 7

A window will appear, prompting you to upload your artwork, name and describe it. Creating a folder for your freshly formed NFTs is all that is required for this step.

Step 8

It will appear as shown below once you've assigned an image to your collection. After that, click the pencil icon in the top right corner to add a banner image to the page.

Step 9

You're now ready to make your first NFT. Use your wallet to sign another message by clicking the blue "Add New Item" button.

Step 10

You can upload your NFT picture, music, GIF, or 3D model in a new window. You can also incorporate specific qualities and qualities to boost the rarity and uniqueness of your NFT on OpenSea and many other markets. Even better, creators can incorporate unlockable content that the purchaser can only access. Passwords to particular services, discount codes, and contact information are all examples of this.

Step 11

When you're finished, click the "create" option at the bottom of the page and sign another message in your wallet to confirm the creation of the NFT. After that, the artwork should be added to your collection.

CST OF MAKING NFTS

While making NFTs on OpenSea is free, other platforms demand a fee. This cost is referred to as "gas" on Ethereum-based systems. The quantity of ether necessary to accomplish a certain action on the blockchain — in this case, adding a new NFT to the marketplace – is known as Ethereum gas. Gas prices vary according to network congestion. The price of gas costs rises in proportion to the number of users transacting value through the network at any one moment, and vice versa.

Top tip: When fewer individuals exchange value across the network during the weekend, Ethereum gas costs are much lower. If you're selling many NFTs, this can help you save money.

HOW TO BUY NON-FUNGIBLE TOKENS (NFT)

Before you go out and purchase NFTs, there are four things you should think about:

- What market will you use to purchase the NFTs?
- To connect to the site and buy NFTs, you'll need to download a wallet.
- To finalize the sale, which coin do you need to fund the wallet with?
- Is it possible to purchase the NFTs you desire at a certain moment, such as during a pack or art drop?

As you may have guessed, certain NFTs are only accessible on different platforms. To buy NBA Top Shot packs, for example, you'll need to register with NBA Top Shot, establish a Dapper wallet, and fund it with either the USDC stablecoin or supporting fiat money. You'll also have to wait for one of the card pack drops to be revealed and hope that you can get one before they sell out.

Pack and art drops are becoming more popular as a way to offer rare NFTs to a large audience of eager buyers. Users are usually required to join up and pay their accounts before the drop to avoid missing out on the chance to acquire NFTs. Pack and art drops may happen in a matter of seconds, so be prepared ahead of time.

BYING NFT FROM RARIBLE

Non-fungible tokens are available for purchase on many NFT markets, including Rarible, OpenSea, and Enjin Marketplace.

Here's how you can get your hands on some through Rarible:

Step 1

Go to the Rarible website and click the 'Connect' button in the upper right corner. Select the wallet you wish to link to the platform and log in from here. Before you can log in, you must agree to the terms of service.

Step 2

After logging in, search the platform for the NFT you want to buy. After you've decided on the NFT you want to buy, click the 'Buy now' option.

Step 3

A confirmation window will display, requesting that you double-check the order's details. If you're ready to go, click the 'Proceed to payment' option to proceed to the next step.

Step 4

Your wallet will then prompt you to confirm the transaction. If you want to proceed, just confirm the transaction, and it will be executed. Your NFT will be sent immediately to your Ethereum address and will be yours to keep once it has been validated.

Please keep in mind that if you buy your NFTs during peak times, you may end up paying a high gas fee.

THE WAVES IN NFT SPACE

A significant new market for NFTs is the manufacture of digital collectibles, which, like traditional trading cards, derive their value from scarcity. As a result, numerous businesses have begun licensing their material for use in digital collectibles, with Terra Virtua at the forefront of the movement.

Terra Virtua advertises itself as the "home of digital treasures," allowing fans to build a digital "Fancave" in which to showcase their NFT valuables. The business published a line of licensed NFTs inspired by the Godfather film trilogy in September of this year.

Gary Bracey, CEO of Terra Virtua, told Decrypt that Terra Virtua's "primary purpose is to deliver NFTs to the public" and that the usage of NFTs was motivated by an idea to merge the digital and real worlds. "We began to think about building something a bit more dynamic—the major driver being to deliver something in the digital world that was not practicable in the "real world," Bracey remarked.

SuperRare

While Terra Virtua makes NFTs inspired by famous companies and Hollywood, other NFT markets specialize in art, another important NFT sector.

SuperRare is a key participant in the growing NFT-powered digital art market. SuperRare, as the name suggests, is all about offering a marketplace for rare and precious works of digital art. Artists' work on SuperRare is validated on the Ethereum blockchain, confirming its worth. According to the SuperRare website, individuals have gathered over 11,000 pieces of artwork thus far.

SuperRare is generating significant business even though it only accepts a "limited number of hand-picked artists," according to its website. SuperRare announced $4 million in artwork sales on its site in October 2020, with artists earning $4.6 million after selling over 11,000 artworks.

Decentraland

NFTs are also gradually making their presence known in the gaming industry. Decentraland is the first completely decentralized gaming universe based on the ERC-20 token MANA. Users may use MANA to purchase products, services, and 10x10m pieces of virtual land, which are supported by the non-fungible LAND token. Decentraland's initial coin offering (ICO) for the MANA token raised $20.7 million and sold out in five minutes. A later LAND sale saw users spend 161 million MANA to purchase virtual plots—roughly $15 million at current pricing.

The game environment is similar to Minecraft. It has basic blocky visuals and user-generated creations ranging from art galleries (where NFTs may be shown) to basic games developed inside the game world.

In addition to LAND, Decentraland supports various other NFTs, such as Axie Infinity and the ever-popular CryptoKitties.

NFTs and Defi

Non-fungible tokens are also making waves in the decentralized finance (Defi) field, which is one of cryptocurrency's most exciting and creative spaces.

Aavegotchi, an experimental business backed by Defi money market Aave, is one example of how NFTs are being utilized in Defi. Aavegotchis are NFT crypto-collectibles utilized in a gaming world; each Aavegotchi also includes Aave's tokens invested within them as collateral, which means that each creates Aave yield. If the owner sells their interest, the Aavegotchi disappears.

Rarible, a decentralized application (or dapp) that allows users to sell digital artwork in the Rarible market, is another application that aims to unify the Defi and NFT communities.

RARI, a governance token intended to reward creators

and collectors, was announced by Rarible in July 2020; it can only be gained by active involvement on the platform, a practice Rarible refers to as "marketplace liquidity mining."

Rarible's market is massive in comparison to other marketplaces. Rarible has dominated NFT sales since September 2020, according to Dune Analytics statistics.

If Rarible maintains its dominance in this industry, Defi will become associated with non-fungible tokens. The NFT business may be developing, but for some, it is ripe with opportunity.

"The race hasn't truly begun yet; this is merely a warm-up," Bracey previously told Decrypt.

RECENT ADVANCEMENTS

The NFT sector increased gradually in 2020, according to a January 2021 study from DappRadar, with daily activity across blockchain games increasing by 35% in 2020 to about 28,000 daily unique active wallets. In addition, Rarible, an NFT marketplace, received $1.75 million in venture financing from renowned industry names like Coinbase Ventures in February 2020.

Meanwhile, NFTs started to change hands for exorbitant prices. First, teen artist FEWOCiOUS sold NFT artwork for tens of thousands of dollars; a Sorare trading card of soccer player Kylian Mbappé sold for nearly $65,000, and a Nifty Gateway auction of digital artist Beeple's work saw one bidder pay $777,777 at the last second for a collection of pieces; a 24x24 pixel image sold for $176,000. Then, in February 2020, an Ethereum startup called Hashmasks sold 16,000 pieces of NFT art for $9 million, bringing NFT mania to unprecedented heights.

Big money was accompanied by even greater names, as musicians and celebrities jumped at the chance to profit. NFTs were founded by rapper Lil Yachty, Rick & Morty creator Justin Roiland, DJ deadmau5, and YouTuber Logan Paul.

A LOOK INTO THE FUTURE OF NON-FUNGIBLE TOKENS

For the time being, much of the emphasis on non-fungible tokens is on artwork, gaming, and crypto collectibles. However, recognizable businesses are increasingly licensing their material for NFTs; fantasy soccer game Sorare has signed up 100 football teams to its platform, while the Smurfs, Minecraft, and the BBC's Doctor Who have all been recreated as NFTs.

Non-fungible tokens could be used in gaming to represent in-game items such as skins, allowing them to be ported to new games or traded with other players.

Their applicability to copyright and intellectual property rights, tickets, and the selling and trade of video games, on the other hand, has far broader potential.

Non-fungible tokens can be used to produce security tokens and the tokenization of both digital and physical assets. For example, like real estate, physical assets might be tokenized to allow for fractional, shared ownership. If these security tokens are non-fungible, the asset ownership is traceable and apparent, even if just tokens representing a portion of the ownership are sold.

Non-fungible tokens might also be used for certification,

such as qualifications, software licenses, warranties, and even birth and death certificates. A non-fungible token's smart contract immutably validates the recipient's or owner's identity and may be placed in a digital wallet for ease of access and representation. Our digital wallets may one day include documentation of every certificate, license, and asset we hold.

BUYING NFT FROM OPENSEA

OpenSea is a peer-to-peer marketplace for digital artworks and crypto-collectibles based on Ethereum. It is the biggest NFT hub, with millions of NFTs from various DApps, including the best-selling ones you've undoubtedly heard of, such as NBA Topshot, CryptoPunks, and CryptoKitties.

There are already over 700,000 virtual assets on the buzzing online marketplace, all of which can be sorted by kind, price, and date of release.

Purchasing an NFT on OpenSea is surprisingly straightforward, especially for beginners. There will be no intimidating strings of words in the process of obtaining your NFT. To utilize the site, all you need is an Ethereum wallet and some cryptocurrency.

Now, let's go through the steps of purchasing an NFT on OpenSea.

Step 1

In your Trust Wallet DApp Browser, go to opensea.io.

Step 2

Select 'Browse' and then 'Filter by' the metrics you want to see.

Step 3

Go through the options and choose your favorite card.

Step 4

Click Buy Now, then go to Checkout after adding funds (ETH) to your wallet.

Step 5

Finally, you complete your purchase by signing the transaction using your Ethereum wallet.

You'll be able to see the NFT you bought on your OpenSea account and in Trust Wallet's "Collectibles" dashboard.

HOW TO SELL NON-FUNGIBLE TOKENS (NFT)

To sell your NFTs, go to the asset page for one of your goods that is visible to the public and tap Sell (you can get there via your account page or by clicking the assets under the search bar you see above). Set your pricing for either a fixed-price listing or an auction. When you're satisfied, click Post Your Listing and follow the on-screen instructions. If this is your first experience selling on OpenSea, you will be charged a gas fee before you can list. Due to Ethereum network congestion, this transaction, which establishes a personal trading smart contract for your wallet, is now pricey, but you only have to perform it once.

If you want to list the things in a currency other than ETH, you'll be asked to authorize the token for trade, which comes with a separate (much lower) gas cost. This is a one-time cost, so you won't have to pay anything the second time around.

You'll be asked to authorize WETH (Wrapped ETH, which is used for making offers on OpenSea) as well as the pay gas cost for accepting the offer if you're going through this procedure for an item you haven't previously advertised. For fixed-price ads, buyers pay the gas, while sellers pay when accepting bids.

If the market is crowded and the transaction is taking too long, you can exit the website and return later. Then, if you go to re-set the listing, the system will recognize that your wallet has completed the transaction, and you will not be asked to pay any fees.

STEP-BY-STEP GUIDE TO INVEST IN NON-FUNGIBLE TOKENS (NFT)

Step 1: Create an account on the NFT Marketplace.

You can browse around an online NFT marketplace without having to register. You'll need to open a digital wallet and fund it with Bitcoin. Your account will be created once you add the digital wallet to the online marketplace. You may then join in the marketplace and invest once it is up and running.

Step 2: Create a Digital Wallet to Buy NFTs

A digital wallet is similar to a physical wallet in that it stores your money, but it is intended expressly to store cryptocurrencies.

In general, a digital wallet that stores your bitcoin on a thumb drive or other physical media, also known as a cold wallet, is the best option. It's less probable that the wallet will be hacked since it won't be active on the internet.

You'll need a digital wallet that's compatible with the NFT marketplace where you wish to invest (for example, Open Sea works with Ethereum). In addition, the cryptocurrency you wish to purchase and sell on the site requires that your wallet be compatible with it. Ether, for example, is supported by MetaMask.

Step 3: Fund Your Account

To engage in an NFT marketplace, you must first purchase a cryptocurrency such as Ether.

Investment brokers that support cryptocurrency trading, such as Webull and SoFi Active Invest, can let you do so fast and simply. Individual equities, exchange-traded funds (ETFs), and options may all be traded without paying a fee. However, you may use them to buy famous cryptocurrencies like Ether and Bitcoin.

Check out Gemini if you're looking for a specialized cryptocurrency platform. It's a full-featured cryptocurrency exchange that allows you to purchase, sell, and store your digital assets. In addition, being a crypto-specific site, Gemini provides a wealth of tools and research data to assist you better understand the cryptocurrency market.

You may load your cryptocurrency into your digital wallet and utilize it on an NFT marketplace after you've purchased it.

Step 4: Purchase your NFT

You'll be ready to purchase once your digital wallet is operational and funded with cryptocurrency.

It's crucial to know that NFT markets employ auction structures. First, you'll have to place a bid on the token you wish to buy. Then, if you are the highest bidder or the only bidder, the transaction will go through.

MINTING NON-FUNGIBLE TOKENS

Many NFT platforms enable you to list and sell NFTs as well. For example, to sell your NFTs on OpenSea, go to the asset page for that NFT and click the "sell" button. You will be able to select the type of sale, such as a fixed price, an auction, or a bundled sale, as well as other terms. On Mintbase, all NFTs are automatically placed for sale. If you did not choose to list an NFT for sale, you can still go to it, check "is for sale," and set a price. The Foundation specializes in NFT auctions. To sell your NFT in an auction, navigate to it, set a reserve price, and then click "List Your NFT" to begin the auction. Auctions last 24 hours, with any bids placed within the last 15 minutes extending the auction by another 15 minutes.

Many creators emphasize curating since they do not want their NFTs to be placed alongside unrelated NFTs by other artists in the same marketplace or virtual gallery. Displaying unrelated NFTs together may also have a detrimental impact on your NFTs' price discovery. Because Dshop already allows the selling of NFTs, all you have to do is create your own Dshop and offer your NFTs for sale on your private store and domain.

NON-FUNGIBLE TOKENS INVESTMENT RISKS

The most significant danger of investing in an NFT is that you will not be able to sell it for the price you paid for it. Even worse, you may not be able to sell it at all.

NFTs should be regarded as valuable collectibles. It's possible that a token, whether purchased or created, may be difficult to sell. It's possible that there isn't a market for it right now. However, if events and trends boost its worth, there may be a market for it in the future.

This is why you should only put as much money into NFTs as you can afford to lose. Making your own NFTs could be a better option. Because creating your tokens will cost you little or nothing, whatever money you make from a sale will be pure profit.

NON-FUNGIBLE TOKEN (NFT)
USE CASES

There have been several speculations on the blockchain uses of non-fungible tokens throughout the years. The fact of NFTs, on the other hand, is that they can provide evidence of genuine ownership of certain assets on blockchain. Furthermore, individuals' rights to certain assets may be held, denied, or restricted by NFTs, guaranteeing exclusivity for the owner. As a result, NFTs have a long future ahead of them, and their applications will INCREASE.

However, in the present day, NFTs are seen as advantageous in a broad range of corporate blockchain use cases. Their capabilities for faster verification of originality and scarcity of information on digital platforms are not to be underestimated. With that said, let us take a closer look at the various non-fungible token use cases listed below.

ART

The recent news of digital artist Beeple selling an NFT of his artwork at Christie's auction for a stunning $69 million sent vibrations across the blockchain world. The record-breaking NFT auction was the culmination of a series of increasingly expensive auctions. Beeple sold his first batch of NFTs in October, with a pair going for $66,666.66. Following that, he sold a number of his pieces for a total of roughly $3.5 million. Christie's, a 255-year-old auction house, places a real value on Beeple's art as well as NFT as a technology.

The most frequent non-fungible token use case is programmable art, which combines creativity and technology. Various limited edition artwork works are now in circulation. Surprisingly, they enable programmability to make changes in diverse situations. The use of smart contracts and oracles may allow artists to create images that can adapt to price variations in blockchain-based digital assets.

As a result, non-fungible token use cases might appeal to the area of legacy arts via tokenization of real-world assets and other works of art. For example, people may simply scan a code on a tag affixed to artwork and register their ownership of the artwork on blockchain using the combined capabilities of blockchain and IoT. Following that, visitors may explore the artwork's whole history, including prior prices paid for it and ownerships.

FASHION

Blockchain has seamlessly integrated into the world of fashion, ensuring benefits to all supply chain participants. Consumers may quickly digitally verify the ownership information of their purchases and accessories, lowering the danger of counterfeiting fraud. Users might simply scan a simple QR code on the price tags of clothing and accessories in the form of an NFT.

As a result, consumers may obtain a clear impression of details such as the location where the content was developed. Furthermore, customers may be able to learn about the persons who had the item before the client acquired it. The use of blockchain technology in the fashion industry has played a critical role in lowering carbon dioxide emissions. As a consequence, they may improve staff well-being while also safeguarding customers. As a result, NFT can develop a new form of blockchain for the supply chain in the fashion industry.

CERTIFICATIONS AND LICENSES

NFT use cases can also provide significant advantages when it comes to verifying licensing and certifications. Like any other degree or license, course completion certificates are often provided to successful candidates in either digital or paper-based format. Before offering a position in a firm or institute, universities and businesses want duplicates of the course completion certificate as references.

Admins might save a lot of time by combining such licenses with NFT functionality. NFT certificates and licenses relieve the load of record checking and verification. As a result, the approach provides a simpler way for keeping proof of course completion or licensing.

COLLECTIBLES

Collectibles are also a significant entry among non-fungible token use cases. In fact, online collectibles like Cryptokitties were one of the first ways people learned about the usage of NFTs. Cryptokitties sprang to prominence in 2017 as they clogged the Ethereum network.

They are essentially one-of-a-kind digital kittens that users may breed to create one-of-a-kind kittens. Each crypto cat has unique characteristics, such as hair texture or eye color, that make them more desirable than others. Users may buy two distinct cats, a Sire and a Dame, for breeding by clicking on a button.

The resulting new kitten has its own identity as well as a Genetic Algorithm, or GA. Thus, the value of crypto-cats is determined by the scarcity of genetic composition. Furthermore, the number of times a Sire is used for breeding other kittens is an important factor in establishing the value of crypto kitties.

SPORTS

Some of the most serious concerns facing the sports industry are counterfeit tickets and merchandise. Blockchain technology provides ideal solutions for addressing such difficulties without hassles. The immutability of blockchain technology aids in the prevention of counterfeit items and tickets.

The example of blockchain-issued tokenized sports game tickets shows how NFT use cases might assist the sports sector. Every ticket is the same, and they all include data that is unique to the ticket's registered owners on blockchain. Sport NFTs are also becoming popular, with several successful athletes' tokenization on the blockchain. The worth of tokens representing successful athletes is determined by their performance.

UNSTOPPABLE DOMAINS AND ETHEREUM NAME SERVICE

Crypto addresses are presented as NFTs via Ethereum Name Service and Unstoppable Domains. Myname.crypto and myname.eth are two famous instances of non-fungible token applications. A user's crypto address is comparable to his or her Twitter or Instagram handle, with each name being unique.

Hundreds of individuals may attempt to get the same handle name if the name is very prevalent. Although Twitter and Instagram prohibit users from selling their username handles, Unstoppable domains and ENS can assist in the flexible buying and selling of crypto addresses. In general, popular names have a higher value than less popular names.

Having said this, it is obvious that non-fungible token applications are gaining traction across a wide range of industries. Since releasing a test version of crypto cats in 2017, NFTs have grown considerably. The gaming industry is one of the most active, with the most active NFT use cases.

At the same time, other industries are gradually embracing NFTs by assuring blockchain integration and asset tokenization. As a result, industries may now use NFT tokens to adopt blockchain, which significantly benefits the token's expanding popularity. Furthermore, the increasing usage of blockchain will also drive the future usage of NFTs as a secondary measure for storing personal data on blockchain or selecting a crypto address. As a result, NFTs have the potential to usher in a future in which people use blockchain and cryptocurrencies in everyday chores without even recognizing it.

❦ 9 ❦

THE CRYPTO MARKET

UNDERSTANDING CRYPTOCURRENCY

In a nutshell, bitcoin is a new type of digital money. You can digitally transmit traditional, non-cryptocurrency money such as the US dollar, but this is not the same as how cryptocurrencies work. When cryptocurrencies become more widely accepted, you may be able to use them to make electronic payments the same way you can with traditional currencies.

What distinguishes cryptocurrencies, though, is the technology that powers them. "Who cares about the technology underlying my money?" you may ask. I'm solely concerned about how much of it is in my wallet!" The difficulty is that the world's present money systems are riddled with flaws. Following are some examples:

- Credit cards and wire transfers are antiquated payment methods.
- In most cases, a slew of intermediaries, such as banks and brokers, take a piece of the action,

making transactions expensive and time-consuming.
- Global financial disparity is increasing.
- Approximately 3 billion individuals are unbanked or underbanked and have no access to financial services. That equates to roughly half of the world's population!

Cryptocurrencies hope to solve some of these issues, if not all of them.

UNDERSTANDING THE BASICS

You know that your regular, government-issued cash is kept in banks. And that you need an ATM or a bank connection to receive more of it or transfer it to others. Well, with cryptocurrency, you might be able to do away with banks and other centralized middlemen entirely. This is because cryptocurrencies rely on a decentralized technology known as blockchain (meaning no single entity is in charge of it). Rather, each computer in the network confirms the transactions.

CRYPTOCURRENCY HISTORY

Bitcoin was the first cryptocurrency ever created! You've undoubtedly heard of Bitcoin more than anything else in the crypto business. Bitcoin was the first blockchain product, which was created by an unnamed individual known as Satoshi Nakamoto. Satoshi Nakamoto proposed Bitcoin in 2008, describing it as a "purely peer-to-peer version" of electronic money.

Although Bitcoin was the first official cryptocurrency,

numerous attempts to create digital currencies years before Bitcoin were formally released.

Mining is the method through which Bitcoin and other cryptocurrencies are produced. Mining bitcoins, unlike mining ore, requires powerful computers to solve complex issues.

Until 2011, Bitcoin was the only cryptocurrency. Then, as Bitcoin enthusiasts began to notice weaknesses in it, they decided to build alternative coins, commonly known as altcoins, to improve Bitcoin's design in areas such as speed, security, privacy, and others. Litecoin was one of the earliest altcoins, aiming to be the silver to Bitcoin's gold. However, there are over 1,600 cryptocurrencies accessible at the time of writing, with the number projected to grow in the future.

SOME BENEFITS OF CRYPTOCURRENCY

Still not persuaded that cryptocurrencies (or any other form of decentralized money) are preferable to conventional government-issued currency? Here are a few solutions that cryptocurrencies, because of their decentralized nature, may be able to provide:

Reducing corruption

When you have a lot of power, you also have a lot of responsibility. When you give a lot of power to just one person or entity, the odds of that person or thing misusing that authority grow. According to Lord Acton, a 19th-century British statesman, "Power corrupts, and absolute power corrupts absolutely." Cryptocurrencies seek to address the issue of absolute power by sharing authority among many persons or, better yet, among all network participants. That is, after all, the basic concept of blockchain technology.

Eliminating extreme money printing

Governments have central banks, and when faced with a significant economic situation, central banks can simply print money. This is also known as quantitative easing. By printing additional money, a government may be able to pay off debt or depreciate its currency. This method, however, is like putting a bandage on a broken leg. It not only rarely solves the problem, but the harmful side effects can sometimes outweigh the initial issue.

When a country, such as Iran or Venezuela, issues too much money, the value of its currency plummets, causing inflation to spike and citizens to be unable to afford basic goods and services. Their money is worth about as much as a roll of toilet paper. In addition, most cryptocurrencies have a fixed number of coins accessible. When all of those currencies are in circulation, there is no straightforward method for a central entity or the firm behind the blockchain to simply generate more coins or add to its supply.

Giving people charge of their own money

With traditional cash, you essentially hand over complete authority to central banks and the government. If you trust your government, that's fantastic, but keep in mind that your government can easily freeze your bank account and refuse you access to your funds at any time. For example, in the United States, if you die without a valid will and own a company, the government inherits all of your assets. Some governments may even simply discontinue issuing banknotes as India did in 2016. As a result, you and only you have access to your funds when using cryptocurrency. (Unless someone snatches them from you.)

Cutting out the middleman

When you transfer traditional money, an intermediary, such as your bank or a digital payment firm, gets a percentage. With cryptocurrencies, all network members in the blockchain serve as the middleman; their compensation is structured differently from that of fiat money middlemen, and so is small in contrast.

Serving the unbanked

A large section of the world's population has no or limited access to payment systems such as banks. Cryptocurrencies hope to alleviate this problem by extending digital commerce worldwide, allowing anyone with a mobile phone to make payments. And, yes, mobile phones are more widely available than banks. In fact, more people own smartphones than toilets, but blockchain technology may not be able to solve the latter issue at this time.

VARIOUS MYTHS ABOUT CRYPTOS AND BLOCKCHAINS

During the 2017 Bitcoin frenzy, several misconceptions about the entire sector began to increase. These fallacies could have contributed to the bitcoin fall that followed the spike. It's crucial to remember that both blockchain technology and its consequence, the cryptocurrency market, are still in their infancy, and things are moving quickly. Let me clear up some of the most common misunderstandings:

Cryptocurrencies are good only for criminals.

Anonymity is one of the key features of some cryptocurrencies. That is, your identity is not revealed when you conduct transactions. In addition, other cryptocurrencies are based on a decentralized blockchain, which means a central government does not solely control them. These characteristics make such cryptocurrencies appealing to criminals; nevertheless, law-abiding residents in corrupt countries can also gain from them. For example, if you don't trust your local bank or nation due to corruption or political instability, blockchain and cryptocurrency assets may be the best way to keep your money safe.

All cryptocurrencies allow for anonymous transactions.

Many people, for whatever reason, associate Bitcoin with anonymity. However, Bitcoin, like many other cryptocurrencies, does not have any form of anonymity. All transactions involving these cryptocurrencies are recorded on the public blockchain. Some cryptocurrencies, such as Monero, value anonymity, which means that no one outside of the transaction can determine the source, amount, or destination. Most other cryptocurrencies, including Bitcoin, do not work in this manner.

Bitcoin is the sole application of blockchain technology.

This couldn't be further from the truth. Bitcoin and other cryptocurrencies are a minor side effect of the blockchain revolution. Many people believe Satoshi built Bitcoin solely to demonstrate how blockchain technology can operate. However, practically every industry and business in the world may benefit from blockchain technology.

Every transaction on the blockchain is private.

Many individuals mistakenly believe that blockchain technology is not available to the general public and is only available to its network of common users. Although some businesses construct their private blockchains for usage only by staff and business partners, the bulk of blockchains underlying popular cryptocurrencies such as Bitcoin are open to the public. As a result, anyone with a computer can view the transactions in real-time.

Risks

Cryptocurrencies, like anything else in life, come with their own set of risks. Whether you trade cryptocurrency, invest in it, or just keep it for the future, you must first evaluate and understand the dangers. Volatility and a lack of regulation are two of the most discussed bitcoin hazards. Volatility reached an all-time high in 2017, when the prices of most major cryptocurrencies, including Bitcoin, surged beyond 1,000 percent before plummeting. However, as the cryptocurrency craze has subsided, price fluctuations have grown more predictable, mirroring the patterns of stocks and other financial assets.

Another key concern in the industry is regulations. The irony is that both a lack of regulation and exposure to rules can become risk events for bitcoin investors.

Risks associated with cryptocurrency will be discussed extensively in subsequent chapter.

SOME CRYPTO ESSENTIALS TO KNOW BEFORE JUMPING TO MAKE TRANSACTIONS

Cryptocurrencies exist to make transactions simpler and faster. But, before you can reap these benefits, you'll need to arm yourself with crypto devices, figure out where you can get your hands on various cryptocurrencies, and get to know the cryptocurrency community. Cryptocurrency wallets and exchanges are among the essentials.

Wallets

Some cryptocurrency wallets, which store your acquired cryptocurrencies, are similar to digital payment services such as Apple Pay and PayPal. However, they differ from typical wallets in that they come in various formats and levels of protection.

Exchanges

After you've obtained a cryptocurrency wallet (see the prior section), you're ready to go crypto shopping, and one of the greatest places to go is a cryptocurrency exchange. These online web services allow you to use the traditional currency to purchase cryptocurrencies, exchange different types of cryptocurrencies, and even store your cryptocurrency.

NOTE: Storing your cryptocurrency on an exchange is considered high risk because many such exchanges have previously been subjected to cyber-attacks and scams. When you're finished with your transactions, the greatest thing you can do is transfer your new digital assets to your personal, secure wallet.

Exchanges come in a range of forms and sizes. Some function as a middleman, similar to traditional stock exchanges, which crypto specialists say is a slap in the face of the cryptocurrency market, which attempts to eliminate a centralized intermediary. Others are decentralized and provide a service that connects buyers and sellers where they deal on a peer-to-peer basis, but they have their own set of issues, such as the risk of locking you out. The third sort of crypto exchange is called a hybrid, and it combines the features of the previous two types to provide users with a better, more secure experience.

BEFORE YOU JUMP IN, MAKE A PLAN.

You might simply want to acquire some bitcoins and keep them for future growth. Alternatively, you may like to become a more active investor, buying and selling cryptocurrencies regularly to optimize profit and revenue. Regardless, you must have a strategy and a plan. Even if your transaction is one-time and you don't want to hear anything about your crypto assets for the next ten years, you still need to learn how to identify things like the following:

- What to Buy
- When should you buy?
- How much should I spend?
- When is it OK to sell?

The following sections provide a high-level overview of the procedures you must complete before purchasing your first crypto.

Select your cryptos

At the time of writing, there are over 1,600 cryptocurrencies available, and the number is growing. Some of these cryptocurrencies may perish in the next five years. Others may skyrocket by 1,000% or more and may even supplant traditional cash.

NOTE: Because the crypto market is still in its early stages, it is difficult to determine the best-performing cryptos for long-term investments. As a result, you may profit from diversifying across different types and categories of cryptocurrencies to reduce your risk. For example, you can increase your chances of having winners in your portfolio by diversifying across 15 or more cryptos. On the other hand, over-diversification can be hazardous; therefore, you must take careful steps.

Analyze, invest, and profit

After you've narrowed down the cryptocurrencies you're interested in, you must choose the optimal moment to purchase them. For example, in 2017, many people began to believe in the concept of Bitcoin and wanted to participate. Unfortunately, many of those investors misjudged the timing and purchased at the pinnacle of the market. As a result, they were not only able to purchase fewer pieces of Bitcoin (pun intended) but they were also forced to sit on their losses and wait for the next price increase.

Now, I'm not arguing that by reading this book, you'll become some sort of new-age Cryptodamus. However, by evaluating market movements and managing risk properly, you may be able to stack the odds in your favor and benefit handsomely in the future.

10

CRYPTO INVESTMENT

W hether you're a seasoned investor who has been exposed only to investment assets other than cryptos or you're just starting to invest (in anything!) for the first time, you're probably wondering why you should consider including cryptocurrencies in your portfolio. Of course, you've undoubtedly heard a little bit about Bitcoin. You've probably heard of other cryptocurrencies like Ethereum and Litecoin. But what's the big deal about all these strange-sounding coins in the first place? Is Litecoin just a little currency that won't take up much space in your physical wallet? Is a Bitcoin made up of shards of other valuable coins? Why should you put your money into coins?

For many investors, cryptocurrency investment may make sense for various reasons, ranging from basic diversification to more exciting things like joining the revolutionary movement toward the future of how we view money. This chapter will show you some of the most interesting aspects of this new investment on the block.

DIVERSIFYING YOUR INVESTMENT

Diversification refers to the old saying, "don't put all your eggs in one basket." This advice may be applied to almost every situation in life. For example, if you're traveling, don't put all your underwear in your checked-in luggage. Instead, put an emergency pair in your carry-on in case your luggage gets lost. Similarly, if you go grocery shopping, don't only purchase apples. Even though "one apple a day keeps the doctor away," you still need the nutrients found in other types of veggies and fruit.

There are many approaches to investment diversification. First, you can diversify with different financial assets, like stocks, bonds, foreign exchange (forex), and so on. Second, you can diversify based on industry, like technology, healthcare, and entertainment. Finally, you can allocate your investment by having both short-term and long-term investment time horizons.

Adding cryptocurrency to your financial portfolio is simply a means of balancing the portfolio. However, because the cryptocurrency sector is so distinct from traditional ones, diversification may enhance the possibility of maximizing the growth of your portfolio. The cryptocurrency market may respond differently to diverse geopolitical and financial events, which is one of the primary reasons for this increased potential.

In the following parts, I go into more detail by quickly examining some of the conventional marketplaces and comparing them to the cryptocurrency market.

STOCKS

The stock market enables you to profit from the success of other industries. You become a part-owner of the business by purchasing its shares. The more equities you purchase, the larger your share of the pie. And, of course, the greater the risk you face if the whole cake is thrown away.

The stock market is one of the most appealing investment assets. Novice investors may purchase one or two stocks just because they like the company. However, most investors' allure of stock investment is the potential that prices may rise over time, resulting in substantial financial gains. Some stocks will even provide you a regular income stream in the form of dividends.

Regardless, for most companies, dividends paid within a year are insignificant when compared to the rise in stock value, particularly when the economy is doing well.

NOTE: Stocks and cryptocurrencies have the following in common: Price appreciation is usually expected when their respective markets are robust.

But, make no mistake, both markets have terrible days and, in some cases, awful years. Investors may utilize the stock market's rich past to assist them in navigating the future. For example, although it may not always seem so, bad days occur less often than happy days.

However, there are certain drawbacks to stock investment. For instance,

- Stocks are subject to a variety of risks. Even the best stocks contain risks that are difficult to eliminate, such as the following:
- The general state of the economy
- Foreign competition

- Government control and regulations
- Event risk
- Market risk
- Purchasing power risk
- Business and financial risk
- The stock selection procedure may be a headache. You actually have hundreds of stocks to pick from. Predicting how the business will perform tomorrow may be challenging as well. After all, the present price simply reflects the company's current condition or how market participants believe it to be.

NOTE: By investing in the cryptocurrency market, you may be able to balance out some of the preceding risks.

However, the ultimate disadvantage of stock investment is identical to that of crypto investing. They both generate less current income than other assets in general. Several kinds of investments, such as bonds (discussed further below), provide more current income and do so with more assurance.

BONDS

Bonds are sometimes referred to as fixed-income securities. They vary from cryptocurrency and equities in that you lend money to an organization for a length of time and get a set amount of interest regularly. As a result, it is classified as "fixed income."

Bonds, like cryptocurrency and stocks, may provide capital gains. However, capital gains operate a little differently. Bond prices do not usually increase in connection with the firm's earnings since the businesses issuing bonds pledge to repay a set amount when the bonds expire. Instead, bond prices increase and decrease in response to changes in market interest rates.

Another thing that bonds, cryptocurrency, and stocks have in common is that they are all issued by various businesses. In addition, several governmental entities issue bonds. If you simply want to diversify inside the bonds market, you may still pick from various reasonably safe bonds to extremely speculative ones.

Bonds are usually less risky and offer greater current income than cryptocurrency and equities. They are, nevertheless, still vulnerable to several risks. Bond investment has some of the same dangers as cryptocurrency and equities, such as buying power risk, business and financial risk, and liquidity risk. Bonds are subject to an extra risk known as call risk or prepayment risk. Call risk refers to the possibility of a bond being called or retired before its maturity date. If the bond issuer calls its bonds, you'll have to find a new home for your funds.

FOREX

Here's another investment option that may be riskier than cryptocurrency. You purchase and sell currencies when you trade on the forex market. Not cryptocurrencies, but fiat currencies like the US dollar, euro, British pound, Australian dollar, or any other money issued by any government. A fiat currency is a country's legal money issued by the government.

Before Bitcoin became the financial asset's fame in 2017, most people identified cryptocurrencies such as

Bitcoin with the traditional FX market. The term "cryptocurrency" includes the word "currency," and crypto owners planned to use their assets to make payments. However, as I mentioned previously in this chapter, cryptocurrencies share many similarities with stocks. When you trade in the forex market, you are not necessarily looking for long-term capital gains. Even the most widely traded currencies, such as the US dollar, are subject to considerable fluctuation throughout the year. A robust US economy does not always imply a stronger US dollar.

As an investor, your primary role in the forex market is to engage in short-to-medium-term trading activity between different currency pairs. You can, for example, purchase the euro versus the US dollar (the EUR/USD pair). You profit if the euro's value rises in relation to the US dollar. However, if the US dollar value rises above that of the euro, you will lose money.

When opposed to stock and cryptocurrency analysis, analyzing the forex market necessitates a different methodology. When analyzing the currency markets, you should consider the issuing country's economic status, upcoming economic indicators such as GDP (or the value of commodities produced inside the country), unemployment rate, inflation rate, interest rate, etc. its political climate.

However, FX, like the cryptocurrency market, must be traded in pairs. In my Forex Coffee Break online forex education course, I equate these pairings to dancing couples — international couples that push each other back and forth. Traders may profit by guessing which way the pair will go next.

A similar approach may be used in the crypto market. You can, for example, pit Bitcoin (BTC) and Ethereum

(ETH) against each other. You may even trade a cryptocurrency like Bitcoin against a fiat currency like the US dollar and speculate on their worth. However, in these circumstances, you must examine each currency, whether crypto or fiat, separately. Then you must compare their respective values and forecast which currency will win the couple's battle in the future.

PRECIOUS METALS

It's time to compare one of the most recent man-made methods of buying stuff (cryptocurrencies) to one of the oldest! No, I'm not going back to the days of bartering, when people traded products and services to meet their necessities. Instead, in the next parts, I talk about the stuff with bling. Before the invention of paper money, precious metals such as gold and silver were widely utilized to create coins and purchase goods.

NOTE: The precious metals comparison is the best argument when someone tells you cryptocurrencies are worthless because they don't have any intrinsic value.

THE BACKGROUND

People used to barter for things that were of actual worth to their human needs, such as chickens, clothing, or farming services. Lydia's ancient civilization is said to have been among the first to utilize gold and silver coins in payment for goods and services. Consider the first customer who attempted to persuade the vendor to take a gold coin instead of three chickens that could feed a family for a week. This was followed by the introduction of leather money, paper money, credit cards, and, most recently, cryptocurrencies.

Some may claim that precious metals, such as gold, have inherent worth. They are long-lasting. Because they carry both heat and electricity, they have certain industrial uses. I recall using gold and silver in experiments back when I was studying electrical engineering in Japan. To be honest, most people don't invest in precious metals since they can conduct electricity. They purchase them mainly to use as jewelry or currency. Today, the value of gold and silver is mostly determined by market sentiment.

NOTE: Silver is more often used in industry than gold. Silver is utilized in batteries, electrical appliances, medical devices, and various other industrial products. Despite the increased demand, silver is less valuable than gold. Silver, for example, is now trading around $16 per ounce, while gold is trading at or over $1,250 per ounce.

Keep in mind that England did not use gold as its official currency until 1816. (The term "standard of value" refers to the practice of linking the worth of a currency to its value in gold.) The United States eventually came on board in 1913 via its Federal Reserve system. It backed its notes with gold to guarantee that notes and checks were honored and redeemable for gold.

Even though precious metals have no disputable inherent worth, they have long been a popular investment instrument among market players. One of the primary reasons is their historical link to riches. People rush to precious metals when investments such as bonds, real estate, and the stock market fall in value or when the political situation is unclear. Furthermore, individuals like to possess precious metals at this time since they can physically touch them and store them in their houses right next to their beds.

Comparing precious metals to cryptocurrencies

Aside from the fact that you must mine to get precious metals and certain cryptocurrencies, one major similarity between precious metals and cryptocurrencies is that both are uncontrolled. At different periods and in various places, gold has been uncontrolled money. When investors do not trust the official currency, unregulated currencies become more valued, and cryptocurrencies seem to be another illustration of this tendency.

NOTE: There are many risk factors to consider when investing in precious metals. For example, if you are considering purchasing precious physical metals as an investment, you must consider the risk of mobility. Because of their weight, hefty import duties, and the requirement for a high degree of security, transferring precious metals may be costly. Cryptocurrencies, on the other hand, do not need a physical transfer. On the other hand, moving cryptocurrency is considerably faster and less costly, even with a hardware wallet, than moving precious metals.

On the other hand, cryptocurrency values have been more volatile in the short period they've been accessible on the market than all precious metals combined. The market's excitement, in particular, was to blame for the 2017 volatility. However, as cryptocurrency investing becomes more mainstream and more people use it for everyday transactions, crypto prices may become more predictable.

Gaining Capital Appreciation

The increase in the price or worth of cryptocurrencies is referred to as capital appreciation. And it's one of the reasons many investors (and non-investors) want to go on the cryptocurrency bandwagon. Bitcoin's early adopters had to wait years before they witnessed any type of capital appreciation. I was one of the skeptics about the whole thing. Back in 2012, one of my Swiss investor buddies advised me to purchase some Bitcoin.

I arrogantly ignored him – and oh, did I regret it later! When the price of Bitcoin skyrocketed, I began investing in cryptocurrencies. However, with some investigation, I discovered cheaper coins with comparable capital appreciation. In the following parts, I examine the history of capital appreciation for cryptocurrencies and explain their potential for development – a major incentive to consider investing in them.

Historical returns

The majority of the gains in the cryptocurrency market before 2017 were due to market hype. For example, when Bitcoin's price reached $1,000 for the first time in 2013, many individuals purchased it. Soon after, its value plummeted to about $300, where it remained for the next two years. The next significant spike in growth came in January 2017, when the price of Bitcoin exceeded $1,000.

If you had purchased one Bitcoin at $300 at the end of 2015, you would have received $700 in capital appreciation (when the price reached $1,000) by January 2017. But the benefits didn't end there. After breaking over $1,000,

Bitcoin's price rose all the way to almost $20,000 by the end of 2017 before plummeting to a range around $6,000.

For those who purchased (or mined) Bitcoin when it was worth about $300 and hung on to it throughout the volatility, the drop to $6,000 was not a huge issue. This is because, even if they didn't cash in their Bitcoins when the value reached more than $19,000, they had approximately $5,700 in capital gain for every Bitcoin they purchased at $300.

People who purchased Bitcoin at $1,000 and cashed it out at $19,000 at its peak in 2017 would have earned $18,000 for each Bitcoin they held. Those who purchased Bitcoin at $19,000, on the other hand, had to wait on their hands and eat their losses following the collapse.

Many market players link the rise of Bitcoin and other cryptocurrencies to the dot-com boom of the mid-1990s and early 2000s. According to Fortune magazine, from its inception in 2009 to March 2018, Bitcoin had four bear (falling) waves in which values fell 45 to 50 percent before recovering an average of 47 percent. During the dot-com bubble, the Nasdaq composite index saw five of these waves, with average losses of 44 percent followed by 40 percent recoveries. The patterns of trading volume are also uncannily similar.

From its low in 2002, the Nasdaq has obviously rebounded well. Though the history and past performance aren't indicative of future behavior, crypto enthusiasts have reasons to believe that growth potential for cryptocurrencies may be similar to the Nasdaq rebound, if not better.

Huge growth potential

Bitcoin and cryptocurrencies were the year's greatest investing story. Every day, stories of individuals becoming billionaires appeared on CNBC and the Wall Street Journal and New York Times.

However, the price of Bitcoin dropped by 63 percent after January 2018. The media quickly followed suit, declaring that the opportunity had gone, that the Bitcoin bull market had ended, and that the bubble had burst.

This tune was intriguing, particularly because many billionaires were becoming crypto investors at the time. For example, J.P. Morgan CEO Jamie Dimon (who had previously branded Bitcoin a scam and threatened to fire any J.P. Morgan traders found trading Bitcoin) became one of the most active purchasers of a Bitcoin-tracking fund. Bitcoin's price fell by up to 24 percent in the days after Dimon's statements, while J.P. Morgan and Morgan Stanley began buying for their clients at cheap prices at the same time.

This is not an isolated case in the cryptocurrency industry. For example, only eight weeks after criticizing Bitcoin at the World Economic Forum in Davos, Switzerland, in January 2018, labeling it a "bubble," hedge fund giant George Soros authorized his $26 billion family office to begin purchasing cryptocurrencies.

The issue is that most individuals have no idea what's going on in the cryptocurrency market. And the majority have no clue where the price is going next. The majority of those interested in the market take their cues from market noise, making it way easier for the prices to fall when the big movers downplay for their benefit.

When most of the market panics about a decrease in the value of an asset, it is often the greatest moment to stock up on it. The same may be said of the bitcoin market. Once the price of a cryptocurrency with robust blockchain technology bottoms out, there is nowhere for its worth to go except up.

INCREASING INCOME POTENTIAL

Although capital appreciation is one of the most appealing aspects of cryptocurrency investment, you can also take advantage of certain cryptocurrencies that pay dividends comparable to stock market dividends.

A bit about traditional dividends

A dividend is an amount of money paid to shareholders by public businesses regularly. Every year, businesses in the United States pay out billions of dollars in dividends. Yet, many investors (especially young ones) don't pay much attention to dividends despite these numbers. Instead, they prefer capital gains because the rewards can be quicker and can exceed any amount of dividend payment.

NOTE: In the traditional stock market, companies typically pay dividends quarterly. The board of directors of a company determines how much to pay in dividends to shareholders and whether to pay dividends at all. When the stock price isn't doing well, the board of directors may opt to issue dividends. As a result, they choose a higher dividend rate to keep investors interested in purchasing the stocks.

Investors with lower risk tolerance may prefer dividend payments to capital gains because dividend payments don't fluctuate as much as the value of stocks does. Furthermore, if the markets crash as they did in 2008, dividends can provide nice protection. But, of course, the best way to accumulate dividends is to hold onto your assets long-term.

THE BASICS OF CRYPTO DIVIDENDS

During the crypto mania of 2017, many cryptocurrency platforms quickly realized the importance of regular payments to keep investors happy. But these payments can be a bit different from traditional stock dividends. There are numerous ways to create consistent, passive income in the cryptocurrency market. Here are the two most well-liked:

HODLing: No, this term is not a typo for "holding," although it has a similar meaning. It is an acronym that stands for "Hold On for Dear Life." It is the closest payment to traditional dividends. Some cryptocurrencies reward HODLers, who merely buy and store digital currency in their wallets.

Proof-of-stake (PoS): This is a lighter version of proof-of-work in cryptocurrency mining. When you "stake" a coin, it means you put it aside so it can't be used in the blockchain network. If you have a ton of stakes, you have a higher chance of getting paid at a random selection by the network. Staking yields annual profits ranging from 1% to 5%, depending on the coin.

Some of the most popular dividend-paying cryptos in 2018 are NEO, ARK, and exchange cryptocurrencies like Binance and KuCoin.

NOTE: While receiving cash (or digital coins) just for holding onto your assets is pretty cool, sometimes it makes more sense to cash out and reinvest your holdings to get a better return.

FUELING IDEOLOGICAL EMPOWERMENT

Just as oil is the lubricant that allows a machine to operate, blockchain technology is the lubricant that enables the cryptocurrency market. Blockchain is the underlying technology for cryptocurrencies, not to mention one of those breakthrough developments that have the potential to revolutionize nearly every industry in the world completely.

Blockchain can offer so much more as it's aiming to resolve many economic and financial problems in the world today, from dealing with the flaws of the sharing economy to banking the unbanked and underbanked. Here are some of the kinds of social good that come through cryptocurrencies and blockchain technology.

The economy of the future

We live in a time when the *sharing economy* is booming. The sharing economy enables people to rent out their possessions to others. Internet giants such as Google, Facebook, and Twitter rely on the contributions of users as a means to generate value within their platforms. If you've ever taken an Uber or Lyft rather than a taxi or rented a room on Airbnb instead of a hotel, you're a part of the sharing economy crowd.

However, the traditional sharing economy has its issues, such as the following:

- **Requiring high fees for using the platforms.**
- **Harmful to individual users but beneficial to the underlying corporation:** In most cases, the value produced by the crowd isn't equally redistributed among all who have contributed to the value production. All the profits are captured by the large intermediaries who operate the platforms.
- **Playing fast and loose with consumer info:** Some companies have abused their power by getting access to private data without customers knowing.

As the sharing economy expands in the future, its problems will likely become more complicated.

Several companies are creating blockchain-based sharing economy solutions to address these challenges. These platforms are much more affordable to use and provide much-needed transparency. In addition, they limit, and sometimes completely cut out, the need for a centralized middleman.

This shift allows true peer-to-peer interactions, eliminating the 20-to-30-percent transaction fees that come with centralized platforms. In addition, because all centralized systems charge a percentage of transaction fees because all transactions are recorded on blockchains, all users can audit the network's activities.

This approach is possible because of the decentralized nature of blockchain technology, which is ultimately a means for individuals to coordinate common activities, interact directly with one another, and govern themselves in a more trustworthy and decentralized manner.

NOTE: Some cryptocurrency transactions aren't entirely free. In many cases, every time there is a transaction on a blockchain, you have to pay the "network fees," which are funds payable to the blockchain network members who are mining your coins/transactions. Consider the time "wasted" waiting for a transaction to clear (for example, it takes 78 minutes for a Bitcoin transaction to reach consensus), then in reality. Therefore, you may not save anything in fees by going to some blockchain applications.

Blockchain remains the fuel behind the future economy, and cryptocurrencies are a byproduct to pave the way by distributing the global economy.

Freedom from government control of currency

In 2017, the rise of Bitcoin and other cryptocurrencies as a trillion-dollar asset class was fueled by the absence of a central bank or monetary authority to ensure confidence or market conduct. Unlike fiat currencies such as the U.S. dollar and the euro, most cryptocurrencies will never be subject to money printing (officially called *quantitative easing*) by central banks. This is because most cryptocurrencies operate under controlled supply, which means no printing of money. In reality, even when demand is great, networks limit the supply of tokens. For example, Bitcoin's supply will dwindle over time, reaching a nadir around 2140. The supply of tokens is controlled by a timetable contained in the code of all cryptocurrencies.

Translation: The money supply of a cryptocurrency at every given moment in the future can roughly be calculated today.

The lack of government oversight over cryptocurrencies can also assist in reducing the danger of inflation. History has repeatedly shown that when a particular government applies bad policies, becomes corrupt, or is faced with a crisis, the country's individual currency suffers. This fluctuation in the currency value can lead to the printing of more money. Because of inflation, your parents paid less than $1 for a gallon of milk, but you must spend at least three dollars. How awesome would it be if cryptocurrencies can get rid of government-controlled inflation so that your grandchildren won't have to pay more for stuff than you do?

Help for the unbanked and underbanked

Banking the unbanked is one of the noblest problems that cryptocurrencies can solve. "2 billion people in the globe still do not have a bank account," according to Coin-telegraph. The majority of them live in low- and middle-income emerging economies, but even in high-income countries, a considerable number of people are unable to meet their day-to-day financial demands through banks. This means they can't take advantage of the ease, security, and interest that banks offer."

Furthermore, many people are underbanked; they have access to a bank account but not to the financial services that banks may give. Even in the United States, 33.5 million households were unbanked or underbanked in 2015. These people cannot participate in the economic growth cycle because they lack access to savings and credit.

TIP: With blockchain technology, cryptocurrencies can assist the unbanked and underbanked by allowing them to construct their financial alternatives efficiently and transparently. To begin using cryptocurrencies such as Bitcoin and sending and receiving money, all that is required is a smartphone or laptop with an Internet connection.

11

NON-FUNGIBLE TOKEN: THE FUTURE OF MODERN ART

T raditionally, any digital art that is shared, saved, or downloaded on the internet can be easily shared, saved, and downloaded. However, because anyone can use it, there isn't a strong sense of ownership. For example, assume you're an artist, a particularly talented one; you also produce some of the most stunning works of art. However, what about putting your creativity to good use?

You appear to have had no luck with it thus far, at least with most people. However, there is a way to give digital art a sense of individuality using NFTs. It also provides an incentive for good artists to continue producing creative works.

The art industry has a lot of potential for NFTs. However, first and foremost, the market must be regulated. There is currently no rule dictating who is allowed to create NFTs and who is not. Until then, I wouldn't invest in NFT stocks without first waiting for the dust to settle. But don't get me wrong—I appreciate art. I truly believe that this has the potential to change the way art is viewed in our society. However, this is merely my opinion;

the final decision is yours to make. Make certain that you have done your study and research.

HOW NON-FUNGIBLE TOKENS (NFTS) INFLUENCE THE ART WORLD

Big Bang NFT Collectors and Speculators have spent more than $200 million on various kinds of NFT-based collectibles over the course of the year, according to market research from NonFung.com. Before this, a creative digital artist named Beeple sold a piece for a record-setting $69 million at Christie's on March 11th. Copyright protection claims are best understood as computer files combined with verification of ownership, such as a registration paper. They exist on a tamper-proof public ledger, like Bitcoin.

Similar to dollars, each cryptocurrency is fiat; that is to say, each BTC is the same as any other currency. However, unlike NFTs, a Rembrandt or a Picasso's paintings don't have any particular value assigned to them, which can be different from buyer to buyer; the highest bidder determines the set value of each painting. To successfully sell their work in an online virtual asset platform, artists will have to sign up and then 'mint' and submit their details on a blockchain (typically the Ethereum blockchain, a rival platform to Bitcoin). Usually, the answer to your question is between $40 and $200. They can then place their ad on an NFT eBay.

Regardless of their monetary value, the whole project seems ludicrous—wealthy collectors offering sic to eight figures for works that can typically be obtained for free. Critics have characterized the NFT phenomenon as nothing more than a market mania, a pun on "this year's digital game retailer crash," as the recent boom-and-bust experience around GameStop stocks. It attracts a disparate mixture of artists and speculators who desire to cash in on the latest fad.

It might be a bubble. However, today's digital artists, who have been consistently overpromising and under-delivering for years on platforms like Facebook and Insta-gram, have chosen to seek their fortune elsewhere. Artists (authors, musicians, and filmmakers alike) see a practical ability to "own" and "sell" ability" of digital objects.

Artists of all ages and abilities will be given opportuni-ties to meet, connect, and gain a new career path. They put many hours and soul into their work as an artist. If it makes them feel good to be rewarded on an appropriate scale, it is pleasant. Futures could play a central role in achieving the blockchain revolution that has major ramifi-cations for mortgages, health care, and personal data management.

Because it's available at no cost, digital art has long been undervalued. The contribution of scarcity is crucial for artists in creating financial value for their work. For some collectors, it is much more important to possess the original item. Few will pay that much money for cardboard with a picture of Honus Wagner, a legendary Pirate, because of scarcity.

Additionally, sneakheads love involves getting the latest releases from Nike and Adidas, as Martin is said to have bought the sole Wu-Tang Clan album for $2 million two years ago.

It is easier to understand that baseball cards, sneakers, and a Wu-Tang Clan CD can be valued when you can see and touch them, but a food CD in a restaurant, a watch in a waiting room, and a bag of heroin aren't. It is also more difficult to see the significance of creative or digital media since it is easily transmittable.

On the other hand, many digital artists claim that they are paying part for labor and the images. They want the digital artwork to be considered an emerging media form. Eager to discover her passion, she explores the creative possibilities of drawing, who said, "I want you to be able to look at these items and see that they are all unique." We had good value for our investment in the product because the artist had put so much time and effort into it. Now that most of us have spent most of the year in cyberspace, it is becoming increasingly clear to us what the alternative lifestyle is all about. Spending money on virtual items makes sense if you spend almost all of your time in the virtual world.

The digital art era started in 2017 with the releases of Crypto-Kit. Most fans have spent over $32 million in one way or another acquiring, trading, and breeding one-anime-style cartoon cats with widgeon eyes. Fortnight players spent an average of $82 in-real 84 dollars on content each year this year.

At the same time, cryptocurrency values have soared; tech celebrities like Elon Musk and Mark Cuban have made significant investments. However, the sudden rise in the value of Bitcoin in 2017, for instance, such as digital collectibles or non-fungible tokens, shows just how low in mania this particular area is.

When they saw an opportunity, technology entrepreneurs Ducan and Griffin Foster started a platform called Nifty Gateways last March. At the time, NFT (New Form of Technology) art was just becoming popular, but no one wanted to give or sell work with anything new. Ease of use and accessibility gave Nifty an incentive for wider adoption. The project was in such an early stage, and we had no hopes for success. However, due to its wide-reaching appeal, it appealed to many Net-savvy Gallery customers, who were happy to buy and sell $100 million in artwork in the first year. OpenSea and MPlace saw a similar rise in their usage; they normally make up to 15% of their sales in the first month or two.

More and more people and businesses, and celebrities are getting into the act. According to the NBA, NBA official app Top Shot has sold over $390 million in NFT packages since its October release, trade on the digital trading card platform run by Dapper Labs. Gronk, a gridiron superstar, sold over a million trading cards of his Super Bowl touchdown highlights, and the Kings of Leon netted over $2 million after selling only two CDs. The Twitter founder was reportedly asked to reveal his first-ever tweet, and it is expected to go for at least $2.5 million at auction. It has been an orgy of activity in the past few months, with high-energy dramas playing out almost daily.

Perhaps one of his more understated revelations was this: "I am pretty f*cked right now," he quipped after breaking his record for the all-time sale.

He believes that so-called whales, a.k.a. big whales, work in the NFT field (financial news trading) world. This pair of big-money investors and evangelists have a substantial financial interest in anything crypto-related and a great deal to gain from the resultant hype. The Winklevoss brothers invested in Nifty Way more than $700,000 into their cryptocurrency of choice in late 2019 when it was among the top 25 cryptocurrencies by market capitalization.

Whale Daniel Maegaard, an Australian bitcoin trader, has reportedly made $15 million or more since 2017. More specifically, Maegaw has spent and made back millions in digital art and other NFT-based items, like a virtual property in Axinfinity, with more than $1 million of her $1.5 million investment. Initially, Maera saw NFT as a means of accumulating wealth-making mechanism, but he's now become a true fan of work and eagerly posts about new acquisitions and sales. He's particularly fond of one picture called Breaking Bad White, which resembles a pixelated human form; for Maerdy as his social media avatar, he has turned down a million-dollar buyout offer. That reputation is now synonymous with me. What would I be if I ever sold him my services to a company?

But even if an investor regards NFT works as just another investment, he or she is helping artists increase their wallets, too. In psychedelic, glitch digital video, Andrew Benson has been tinkering with it for years. He has worked as a full-time artist for the past twenty years, although he has also done commissions for artists such as MIIAA and Aphex Twin. I have held this belief for many years: To be successful as an artist, the only option is to not be successful as an artist.

It wasn't going well a year and a half ago when his plans to show new videos to the public failed. He wonders, "Do I have to do all this work, then find locations to display it?" Next, his friend at an NFT Foundation organization requested he submits something. He didn't believe it was very creative, but he thought that the Internet was a good way to get more traffic. It will produce a Rorsch in a dynamic, kinetic-colored state of mind for $1,250. Since then, he has been able to place a total of 10 pieces in the same price bracket. Now he wonders if he can become self-support anguished. It shook my worldview. In this instance, it takes me back to thinking like an artist; when I see the work I have created, I find a context and a place where it can have an impact.

Noted creative and open-minded contemporary artists are getting their due from NFT collectors as well. Graphics with whirling 3D scenes, saturated color palettes, and witty cartoons abound in today's world. With a young generation raised on the Instagram app and the masses who have no familiarity with fiat currency, these internet aesthetics are catching the attention of people and Twitter-feed customers. Fintech is something for punks. Although street art and anti-establishment styles help convey that to others, those fintech customers are simply punks in the mainstream.

This is good news for those in the conventional world because they no longer fear for their position in the market. We're at a watershed moment of inflection: the interest and mental energy of the demographic are significantly below that of the beginning of the internet. Rival auction house Christie demonstrated that even if other powerhouses could not grasp the financial benefit of the artist, Pak understood the music genre.

In the absence of the establishment's support, artists of all ages engage in collaborative production in tight-knit NFT-run, single communities, echoing artists from past movements and receiving feedback from each other and generations. This influences their thinking and approach, and output. It's a selfless ethos in the digital arts and design space. Mostly in independent music and fine art, there is a belief that the project will fail unless a single person dominates. There's a feeling of everyone being able to benefit from this.

There are cases where the minnows and the whales are migrating together. It turned out to be a personal collecting group in the $69 million, called the Metapurse, two Singaporean investors models built on cutting-edge technology. In January, the two purchased 20 Beeple works of art, cataloged them in a virtual gallery for free, and divvied the business into a collection of 5,400 tokens. These concepts now have six times their value as of March 16th, 2021. It is speculated that the team will display their latest headline-making acquisition in a state-of-the-art virtual museum. It is to bring the world of art and creativity to everybody's door.

The market for NFTs, with respect to artists, speculators, and collectors, also has a dark side. Some creators might opt out of participating in the action with such high entry costs and technical expertise required. Many fear that younger artists of color will be marginalized within the "traditional white" art world. The legal community is focused on understanding this new development due to the work of artists being copied and sold without their permission. It is giving people new opportunities to profit from other people's work.

Finally, there are environmental issues to be taken into consideration. For example, a considerable amount of computing power is used to create NFTs, and many servers run on fossil fuels. Cryptocurrency experts warn that "the environmental effect of blockchain's distributed ledger technology is enormous," but an adjunct professor of visual arts at New York University disagrees.

There is less impact on the future of the climate with a new blockchain. For instance, they are finding new uses for NFT technology already. Some people, for instance, pay tokens when their performance is broadcast as a second run, like an actor receiving a royalty check every time their show airs on TV. Music rights management startup, Bitmark, has rolled out a new model called NFT-like that will let music producers all over the world receive a share of the profits from their artists' work. In contrast to companies like Facebook and Instagram, which give non-fans rights and do not allow payment, those who join the NFT online communities receive ownership of the platform and make money in the form of direct compensation.

Many technology evangelists continue to believe that digital currency and blockchain platforms can change the world in profound ways, so for them, the latest NFT craze is nothing new in Utah. Blockchain has already been used to protect the voting process at Nationwide Insurance and combat insurance fraud at Optum Health and other organizations. Advocates say that it could help companies create a transparent supply chain by aggregating knowledge, offer joint aid, and lower financial discrimination in lending.

It has so much to offer to society that we should attempt to manage that as much as possible. Unfortunately, in the world of new ideas, everything from new product launches to media, and you can see an "idealarming" improvement followed by a "grotesque failure" syndrome.

12

BECOMING SUCCESSFUL IN THE NFTS MARKET

Making digital art is not a new concept; in fact, it has been around since the early 1980s, when computer developers created an art program utilized by the digital artist Harold Cohen. Nowadays, producing digital art is as simple as opening your paint program or taking a picture with your phone, adding a filter, and then uploading it for everyone to see.

You may already be a digital artist and be unaware of it. You are already an artist if you shoot images on your phone or draw on your paperwork; you simply need to polish your skills.

If you wish to become an NFT artist, you will need to follow some fundamental steps. That being said, being an NFT artist is simpler than you think; but, building a following and being consistent may be difficult.

1. CHOOSE THE KIND OF ART WORK TO CREATE

Before you begin your long and thrilling path of becoming an NFT artist, you need to pick out what type of artwork you are going to make. Having a constant specialization while making your digital art may help you develop your skills and enable your audience to realize what artwork you generate.

For example, if you are an artist who enjoys creating digital images of famous sports stars, your audience will understand that you enjoy sports and create work connected to sports. If one day you decide to produce a digital artwork of a unicorn, though, you may throw your fans off and confuse them. This might either be good or terrible, but it's essential to be constant in your style so people can learn to either love or detest your work.

Choosing your art specialty should be very straightforward. Maybe you already have a specialty you create for fun? It might be nature photos, cats, doodles - the sky is the limit when picking your specialization. My major advice for developing your niche is to select a subject you like creating. If you instead select something that's hot or trendy, you may not experience the success you're searching for.

The amazing thing about NFT art is that you can genuinely make anything into a one-of-a-kind masterpiece. You may produce music, videos, paintings, drawings, images, basically anything! So, be true to who you are and what your interests are, then let your audience determine what they enjoy and what they don't like.

2. CHOOSE HOW YOU WILL CREATE YOUR ART

After determining your art niche, you must select how you will create that art. For example, if you are a nature photographer, you may not need to purchase a picture editing application. However, if you are beginning from scratch or need to make changes to your artwork, you will need to utilize editing software.

- Image editing software: There are a few common solutions among NFT artists if you need to generate or modify digital photos. Adobe Illustrator, Lightroom, and Photoshop are all strong options for picture editing.
- GIF and Pixel Image Creation Software: Adobe Photoshop (GIFs) and Piskel (animated sprites and pixel art)

There is, of course, other software available. But, finally, the sort of software you need is determined by your art style and personal goals for your art pieces.

3. CHOOSE A DIGITAL ART FILE TYPE

Once you've decided what kind of NFT art you're going to make, you'll need to determine what file format you're going to use to create it. There are several file formats for each style of art.

Here is a list of possible digital art file formats for creating NFT art:

CATEGORY
FILE FORMAT
Video
MP4
Image
WEBP, PNG, JPG, GIF
Audio
WAV, MP3
Basically, all you have to do is decide what kind of art

you want to create and then proceed from there, making sure to choose the optimal file format for your purposes. Furthermore, you can always add unlocked content to your NFT art, which means that they will have access to the best quality format you supply when someone buys it. That way, you won't have to produce the token as a big file, which may cause problems loading on certain markets.

4. MAKE YOUR OWN DIGITAL ARTWORK

Now that you've determined your art niche, how you will create your art, and the file format in which you'll save your art, it is time to create your first piece of NFT art!

Keep in mind that your non-fungible artwork does not have to be perfect. Every day, the most important thing you can do is create art. Now, just because you create new art every day does not imply that you must post new art every day. Instead, you should make new art every day for practice and to get your creative juices flowing. Take, for example, the famous NFT artist Beeple, who sold an art piece containing 5000 pieces of his art, which he created daily for over 13 years, for $69 million!

Creating NFT art should be something you enjoy and are passionate about because becoming a successful NFT artist takes time and a lot of patience.

5. MARKET YOUR NFT ART

Things are starting to heat up now! When you're ready to sell your first piece of NFT art, you'll need to decide which marketplace is best for your collection. There are several markets to select from, each with its own set of advantages and disadvantages. Furthermore, as the world of NFTs and NFT art evolves, new markets will emerge.

You can sell your NFT art in the following market-place: SuperRare.co, NiftyGateway.com, Rarible.com, and OpenSea.io.

When initially selling your NFT, my recommendation is to make an account on all of the sites and publish your work to simpler sites like OpenSea and Rarible. You would then apply to be an artist for the other sites that need application evaluation after having some work up and a few pieces (SuperRare and NiftGateway).

Remember: When building your marketplace accounts, be sure to include all of your social media connections and personal websites in your profile. This enables individuals who find you to follow you on social media, so increasing your following.

6. BUILD YOUR FOLLOWING

Okay, this is the most important step. You must amass a following or an audience. There are several methods to establish a following to aid in the promotion of your NFT art; but, what are the greatest methods to build a following?

To gain a following for your NFT artwork, you must create a brand around it or establish your own brand while using your NFT artwork at every step of the way. In addition, participating in the NFT community via forums, podcasts, and blogs can help you create credibility and trust with your audience. Using social media is also a wonderful idea.

This phase is vital since your brand's reputation is critical to your art's worth. The more people who know about you, the more they understand you and what you stand for. This makes it much simpler for both parties to purchase a piece of your artwork. Consider this: would you rather purchase something from someone you know and trust or from a random stranger you know nothing about? The answer is straightforward.

You may use many approaches to establish a loyal following; let's go through some of the best ones.

Social Media

In my view, one of the simplest methods to begin building a following for your NFT art projects is via social media. To make the most of social media, be sure to join as many as you can and make a lot of noise. Once you're up and going, try to publish 1-2 times a day. You should be submitting your artwork and soliciting feedback, as well as providing input to other artists and assisting them whenever possible.

For six months, upload one piece of artwork every day across all of your social media platforms and watch what happens. Using appropriate hashtags to help your social media postings reach the right people can help you attract more followers who interact with your posts, which is precisely what you want.

Here are some trendy hashtags I've spotted on social media that are expected to acquire popularity in the next years. #NFT, #NFTs, #NFTART, #NFTARTIST, #NFTCOMMUNITY, #NFTCOLLECTOR, #CRYPTOCURRENCY, #ETHEREUM, #ETH, #DIGITALART, #DIGITALARTIST, #NONFUNGIBLETOKENS.

When creating your social media account, decide whether you want to use your personal account or create a separate account for your artwork. This is the scenario I mentioned earlier about personal branding vs. product branding. Whatever you choose, make sure to fill out your bios effectively, including details that describe you as an NFT artist, the type of art you create, and links to any other social media accounts or personal websites you may have.

Essentially, you want to build a webbed network so that you can reach people across all platforms. As a result, try to keep your social media names consistent across all platforms; this aids in brand recognition.

Maintaining social media can be time-consuming. That is why it is best to start slowly and not get too caught up in how many followers you have or how many likes your post receives. Instead, just be yourself and focus on providing content. Remember, we all started from scratch. Growing your following takes time, patience, and consistency, but I know you can do it!

Websites

Aside from social media, you might take a more technical approach and build your own website. However, even if you opt to build your own website, it's still a good idea to be active on social media and utilize it to supplement traffic to your website, so people can see what you're giving.

If used correctly, a website may benefit your NFT art. For example, you may showcase your NFT art collection on your website by providing links to your art's marketplace, establishing a blog that attracts organic visitors, or even offering a service like making bespoke artwork for customers or teaching others how to produce their art. The possibilities are limitless.

Finally, if you are competent with computer technology, developing your website is a viable choice for expanding your audience. You may also hire someone to develop a website for you.

7. ENGAGE IN THE NFT COMMUNITY

It's time to tie everything together. It's time to get active now that you've set up your social media accounts and your website (if you have one). Spend time in your community answering questions, asking questions, and taking polls. For example, if you're a Rarible.com or OpenSea.io artist, go to their forums and start reading through the posts. Answer any questions you feel comfortable answering, and if more information is needed, direct them to your blog or a YouTube video you created on the subject. Help others, and they will help you.

Furthermore, never be afraid to ask questions. If you have a question, either figure it out on your own or ask someone in the community. Surely, if you're asking the question, it's very likely that someone else is as well.

Overall, gaining a following requires passion, patience, consistency, and selflessness. First, you must be passionate, patient while remaining consistent and selfless to assist others in solving their problems.

8. MAINTAIN CONSISTENCY

The importance of consistency cannot be overstated. It makes no difference what you do in life; consistency is important. If you intend to become a successful NFT artist overnight, I wish you the best of luck — you'll need it. Without consistency, you have little trust, and no one cares.

You must demonstrate to others that you are serious

about what you do and the NFT art you make. Beeple is a prime example. It took him almost 13 years to achieve significant success, but it was well worth the wait.

You are not giving yourself a fair opportunity if you are not consistent with your work. I suggest sticking with it for as long as you can, but at the very least for six months. If you haven't seen a good trend after six months, it's time to reassess your strategy and go back to the drawing board.

9. BE HONEST AND TRUE TO YOURSELF AND YOUR ART

As if being consistent wasn't difficult enough, you must also ensure that you are always genuine to yourself and the art you create. I bring this up because many individuals get caught up in trends and forget why they began doing NFT art in the first place. Trends aren't inherently bad, but make sure that whatever trend you're following, you still bring your unique spin to your creation.

Being genuine to yourself and your work influences how people see you as an artist and as a person. For example, if you are always jumping on the newest hot artworks, you may be seen as a money-hungry NFT art slanging fiend, and as a consequence, a lack of trust develops.

Furthermore, creating art that you like can help you remain motivated and creative, preferably constantly.

10. NEVER GIVE UP

Obviously, the finest was reserved for last. But, when it comes to your career as an NFT artist, these three simple phrases may make or break you. One of the most popular fallacies among individuals embarking on a new adventure is that success occurs overnight. Sure, some individuals have found rapid success; but, as NFTs progress and become more popular over the globe, your chances of success tend to dwindle.

Don't give up for your own sake. It may take years to build a following that is devoted enough to buy your NFTs regularly, but bear in mind that all it takes is one piece of art to transform your life.

If I could only give you one bit of advice, it would be to enjoy your journey. Your journey serves as the basis for your whole artistic career. In my perspective, it's incredible that every choice you make and every piece of art you create serves as the foundation for your tale. So, if you're feeling down because your work isn't selling, or if someone has said anything negative about it, just keep pushing ahead and keeping your eyes on the goal, and you'll be able to make your goals come true.

Being an NFT artist is a thrilling adventure. Understand that becoming a successful artist, in general, involves time, consistency, and effort. Create your work, get a following, and assist others along the way, and you'll be well on your way to being a successful NFT artist.

13

A LOOK INTO THE FATE OF NFT

The non-fungible tokens (NFT) market in 2020 significantly increased, and the absolute estimation of the arrangement rose 299% year-over-year to more than $250 million. USD, as indicated by another investigation distributed by market examination firm NFT Nonfungible.com. The report, created on the side of the gauging exercises of L'Atelier BNP Paribas, the third yearly NFT market review, showed that NFT is quickly turning into the world's driving resource class in the coming years.

NFTs are blockchain-related computerized resources that are interesting and can't be supplanted by different resources compared to digital forms of money. Models range from virtual plots on multi-client stages to programmable artistry and actual property registers. Since they are exceptional and difficult to repeat, they can overcome any barrier between the virtual and actual economy, giving a tremendous market to important advanced products that can be exchanged, gathered, and exchanged.

The report, which uses patented technology to monitor activity in the NFT market, found that all NFT transaction's total value (including sales and all other operations such as breeding, foraging, and renting) increased from $62,862,687 in 2019. Up to $250,846,205 in 2020.

Also, NonFungible.com significantly increased market activity: the total number of active portfolios conducting NFT transactions (including buying, selling, holding, or using the blockchain program) increased by 97%, from 112,731,209 million to 222,179 in 2020. Similarly, the number of buyers and sellers increased from 44,644 to 74,529 (+66%) and from 25,264 to 31,504 (+24%), respectively. The number of active portfolios accelerated during 2020, indicating even faster growth in 2021: overall growth in the fourth quarter was twice as high as in the third quarter and three times as high as in the second quarter.

SHOWCASE FOR NFTS AND SOCIAL

Showcase (showcase.to) and The Giving Block (thegivingbloxk.com) have joined forces to activate the unique NFT donation campaigns created by Showcase. Showcase creators choose from more than 100 nonprofits partnering with the proceeds from selling their badges to a charity of their choice. In addition, content developers will be able to decide what selling price will benefit a nonprofit organization.

Showcase introduces NFT to the general public using highly adaptable technology developed by Matic Network under the Matic Build-N-Earn Scholarship Program. The Matic Network is an EVM-compatible Plasma-POS hybrid secondary circuit that enables fast operation (5000TPS) at the cost of 1/1000 of the Ethereum network.

Crypto collectibles are selling for thousands, and

famous people like Mark Cuban are trading in cold hard currency.

There is unrest over discussions about digital collectibles in cryptocurrency, unique virtual tokens that can reflect everything from art to sports memories. These NFTs, or irreplaceable tokens, were sold for hundreds of thousands of dollars. Sheldon Corey of Montreal, Canada, told CNBC that he paid $20,000 for one of the thousands of CryptoPunks created by computers.

According to the NFT data tracking tool CryptoSlam, Dapper Labs, in collaboration with the basketball league platform NBA Top Shot, has attracted $147.8 million in the past seven days. This service permits users to buy and sell short clips showing highlights of the most important basketball games.

Mark Cuba and other celebrities profit from the NFT craze. The billionaire owner of the Dallas Mavericks sold digital goods online at auction and owned them himself. The greater impulse of these chips is because bitcoin and other cryptocurrencies have risen sharply in recent months, also at a time when people are spending more time indoors due to coronavirus restrictions.

CASHING ON FUTURE UPSIDE

The basic idea is that by adding an advanced contract that enshrines the rights of the principal issuer of the Token to future revenues from secondary market sales, digital asset developers can be encouraged to relinquish control of it.

In this way, instead of confining players to a fenced-in value-capturing garden, they can allow their wealth to escape to a larger world where they can create greater brand value. There has been a division of discussion about artists doing the same with unique and unique works of art. From now on, an artist can sell a painting to a buyer for $10,000 but will not benefit if the collector or gallery later buys it from the first buyer for, say, $1 million. Supposedly the work is inextricably linked to a unique NFT and a reasonable contract to handle future transaction rights. In that case, the original artist may be a way to participate in that future evaluation.

This method could also allow you to pay for derivative works by creators working with other people's original music or other artistic content. Or it could help charitable efforts such as Project Honu, as reselling a crypt turtle kitten to prospective buyers could continue to donate funds to the philanthropic purposes he represents.

This type of idea makes NFT conversation so engaging that it allows us to break away from existing mental models so that innovators can develop new, creative approaches to problems. So far, much of it is very intangible, although it was good to see NFT. NYC p[participants such as Vault.io demonstrates the ability of commercial NFTs to transform gift tokens, branding, and trade exchanges by showing visitors how to redeem Token in your wallet for a cup of coffee supplied by a Raspberry Pi compatible coffee machine.

THE TENSION BETWEEN COMMUNITY AND ECONOMY

The question remains whether a close community of interest associated with specific NFTs can generate sufficient liquidity to make them viable. This will largely depend on the success of various community blockchain initiatives and interoperability solutions, such as the

Cosmos and Polkadot networks, which could allow NFTs to cross blockchains. If you want the globe to be '\tagged' with these unique digital markers, as some suggest, we have to go beyond the complex processing capabilities of Ethereum and its competitors.

It is a vision worth fighting for, as communities are the ground for the concept of all values. If you can take advantage of it, you can encourage adoption. To achieve this, developers must consider that every community is unique: the things they value, the contracts their members make, and their self-management preferences are not necessarily built into monolithic block circuits. Rigorous programming logic.

That is why, in addition to NFTs, other projects work with community-based digital asset release models that are spine or virtual machine-independent, like Ethereum. Process all transactions. These include Intercoin, now best known for its famous hand-painted murals welcoming drivers on the Gowanus Freeway to Manhattan from Brooklyn, and the Space Agency, a colorful name coined by a group of radical economists in Auckland in California. Technologists and other social scientists.

The general idea of these concepts is that the smart contract's functionalities, the terms attached to the badge, and the contract template can be uniquely designed according to the preferences of each community. The question emerges as to whether they can be protected from attack and sufficiently liquid.

All of this raises the tension between the narrow subjectivity of an individual community's expression of value and the demand to link this otherwise closed subgroup of interests to the universally accepted expression of community value. In general, the economy has convertible and negotiable instruments such as bitcoin or the dollar.

By addressing these tensions and identifying the best business models that will overcome them, NFTs and their examples have the greatest potential for practical and realistic implementation, which can significantly impact the world. The more the people who work there gather and explore perspectives, the greater the chances of success.

PROBLEMS WITH NFTS

The issues with Digital Ownership

For example, at the time, many people thought that a blockchain could be a delivery device to easily transfer digital assets in much the same way as a cryptocurrency with the application of media assets. Block circuits are great as transaction tracking books but terrible as digital asset storage or distribution systems of any size. First of all, the media resource files are just too big. This means that for a digital media asset, the file itself—be it a photo, a video, or an email. A book, or something else, has to "live" somewhere else. In Blockchain, you can create a permanent and secure asset record, and that record can be cryptographically "linked" to an asset wherever it doesn't belong in a chain, but they don't live together. This can cause problems when the main digital asset is deleted or replaced on the platform where it is located.

First sale and "double cost."

Another factor complicating the digital value is that

although the physical objects are not interchangeable, even two copies of the same book will have small differences in their binding, color appearance, book quality. In contrast, digital media can theoretically be infinitely reproducible and not very different. Digital files can be reproduced so easily that U.S. courts have refused to recognize the doctrine of "first digital sales." There is no such thing as multimedia assets under copyright law. A unique digital device can be bought and sold in the aftermarket because media files are essentially treated as replaceable.

NFT rescue (partial)

Because NFTs are digital tokens, they can be purchased to be bought and sold in the market. Just like the cryptocurrencies by which they are modeled. However, it is necessary to hold in mind that none of the NFTs replace the fact that, like library books on shelves not attached to their library cards, the main assets of NFTs exist elsewhere "out of the chain."

14

THE FUTURE OF DIGITAL
CURRENCY

The world is going digital in almost all of its ramifications. The term "digital" is derived from the Latin word "digitus," which means "finger, toe." Now, it is present in computers, music players, wristwatches, cell phones, etc.

And then came the book press, lauded as a liberator by many. Once upon a time, books were available only to the wealthy. We now have e-books and other devices that anyone can use. But, despite being digital and having been converted to words, we still prefer a physical book over a piece of electronic plastic that must be recharged to function.

If you truly believe in the proposition that digital currencies such as bitcoin can make positive change in the world, how? If you want to answer this question, it is important to investigate money regarding how we conceive of a better world for all; and we must ask how we use it, why we do. Unlike other forms of property, I have learned that money can be used before an occurrence even taking place. Its innumerable manifestations and effects imply nothing, yet its only simple meaning is good or bad. It's a special but often misunderstood and underutilized ingredient. This demonstrates that money is neutral when used to buy and sell but complex when applied to other purposes such as ethical or moral decision-making.

It is endogenous and exogenous, in the same way, at the same time, since it has characteristics that are intrinsic to its culture while at the same time is dependent on the global community.

The device lacks an identity and can be easily replaced, yet it is seen as a non-renewable asset within the broad context. However, as a matter of principle, results are never entirely predictable, and if you want to use it, it may not be an essential requirement.

A currency must be believed to have inherent value by those who hold it. In November 2013, the United States Senate Committee on Homeland Security and the government agreed that recognizable monetary forms, such as Bitcoin, are a legitimate form of revenue. Migrant laborers can utilize the 'Bitcoin organization' to send cash to their families without giving them high charges because of low exchange expenses. A European Commission estimated that if the global fee for remittance is lowered to 5% (which the G20 backed in 2011), an additional $15 billion could be supplied to developing countries. These money transfer services could be dis-intermediated through an infrastructure-based system.

Cryptocurrencies are unique in that they are both distributed and decentralized. Because of the internet, we may only see the 'tip of the iceberg' discoveries of new applications that will give rise to undiscovered marketplaces. To function more efficiently, in the past, the corporation had to entrust control to a large number of people;

today, the dependency on a network has opened the door to the "ability network power" up to a small number of elites with dominant interests.

It has been said that Bitcoin is money's move to decentralization, and it may be considered to be a more streamlined system approach. Thus, Bitcoin represents a paradigm shift equal to file-sharing peer-to-peer and telephony (e.g., Skype).

Almost no regulations have been established for digital or virtual currencies, but existing laws can differ greatly according to each jurisdiction's financial regulations: taxation, stock, securities, criminal, or civil rights, pensions, commodities, social security, consumer protections, etc.

The two primary problems that bitcoin faces are whether it is an asset. There are several currencies in the world that are expressly made in another country's money (for example, the US dollar, which the government recognizes). In addition, Germany allows the usage of units of a priori of account that are commonly regarded as private money as a world leader in the effort to reduce transaction costs.

Under the first scenario, the obvious disparity is that, unlike tangible property, digital currencies can be divided into many small parts, albeit briefly, which is not immediately obvious. When a country's economy is developed, that generally means it has made it inordinately easier for digital currencies to thrive.

Capital-controlled economies are implicitly antagonistic because they can effectively be defined as having control of their money supply. It is evident that the value of bitcoin cannot be realized through democracy since it is subject to market forces, which can impact our social objectives. However, any new cryptocurrency could implement more egalitarian monetary policies, financial and governance models.

So what if a "digital currency" could make a real contribution to those social issues, such as inclusive culture, equal opportunity, or mutualism; wouldn't those be positive contributions? In addition, the emergence of virtual currencies such as bitcoin has increased the importance of innovation in the cryptocurrency industry.

These factors influence the effectiveness of money in bringing about social and environmental change, whether through political ideology, the economic environment, community aspiration, or individual desire. In cases where a local currency could be created to build a more resilient local economy and enhance socioeconomic well-being, an investigation into a national currency must be undertaken. When the current economic system falters, one can see such symptoms as an increase in social divisions, high crime, decreased physical well-being, low social participation, and an absence of a sense of community.

AFTERWORD

Non-fungible tokens are now dominating the collectibles and digital art sectors. Suddenly, any kind of digital artist is discovering new ways to promote their work and earn a good living from it. Not just digital artists but also celebrities and other global businesses are vying for a place in the digital assets market. The recent record-breaking sale of a non-fungible token or NFT art for $69 million Ethereum is the cause for NFTs' increasing appeal.

Digital artists such as Beeple are now utilizing NFTs to distribute their work, and blockchain can check if the pricing is genuine or not. However, NFTs are not confined to digital art. NFTs may be used for several purposes, including ownership of any rare and unique item, as well as ownership of another type of asset. It may also take physical form; hence NFTs are not limited to digital alone.

Investing in non-fungible tokens differs from investing in cryptocurrency. Every NFT is unique, and it will have a distinctive value and price. So, to purchase and sell NFTs, some kind of media must be linked to them to boost their value.

Because of all the attention paid to NFTs, many people are now perplexed about how they may purchase and sell NFTs. This book has discussed all you need to know about buying and selling NFTs, and we hope it was useful.

REFERENCES

Charles, P. (2021). NFT Guide: How to Create and Sell Non Fungible
  Tokens, discover Crypto Art and Collectibles as Crypto Assets.

John, H. (2021). The Ultimate NFT And Crypto Art Guidebook.

Juan, J. (2021). A Guide to Crypto Collectibles and Non-fungible
  Tokens NFTS: The Beginner's Guide).

Nikita, K., Antorweep, C., & Chunming, R. (2021). Blockchain Based
  Transaction System with Fungible and Non-fungible Tokens for a Community-Based Energy Infrastructure.

Paudel, A. et al. (2018). Peer-To-Peer Energy Trading In A Prosumer-

Based Community Microgrid: A Game-Theoretic Model. IEEE Trans. Ind. Electron.

Pop, C., et al. (2018). Blockchain Based Decentralized Management
Of Demand Response Programs In Smart Energy Grids.

Regner, F., Urbach, N., & Schweizer, A. (2019). NFTs in Practice–
Non-Fungible Tokens as Core Component of a Blockchain-based Event Ticketing Application.